INDEPENDENT READING

SOLVING PROBLEMS IN THE TEACHING OF LITERACY
Cathy Collins Block, Series Editor

Recent Volumes

Tools for Matching Readers to Texts: Research-Based Practices
Heidi Anne E. Mesmer

Achieving Excellence in Preschool Literacy Instruction
Edited by Laura M. Justice and Carol Vukelich

Reading Success for Struggling Adolescent Learners
Edited by Susan Lenski and Jill Lewis

Best Practices in Adolescent Literacy Instruction
Edited by Kathleen A. Hinchman and Heather K. Sheridan-Thomas

Comprehension Assessment: A Classroom Guide
JoAnne Schudt Caldwell

Comprehension Instruction, Second Edition: Research-Based Best Practices
Edited by Cathy Collins Block and Sheri R. Parris

The Literacy Coaching Challenge: Models and Methods for Grades K–8
Michael C. McKenna and Sharon Walpole

Creating Robust Vocabulary:
Frequently Asked Questions and Extended Examples
Isabel L. Beck, Margaret G. McKeown, and Linda Kucan

Mindful of Words: Spelling and Vocabulary Explorations 4–8
Kathy Ganske

Finding the Right Texts: What Works for Beginning and Struggling Readers
Edited by Elfrieda H. Hiebert and Misty Sailors

Fostering Comprehension in English Classes: Beyond the Basics
Raymond Philippot and Michael F. Graves

Language and Literacy Development: What Educators Need to Know
James P. Byrnes and Barbara A. Wasik

Independent Reading: Practical Strategies for Grades K–3
Denise N. Morgan, Maryann Mraz, Nancy D. Padak, and Timothy Rasinski

INDEPENDENT READING

*Practical Strategies
for Grades K-3*

DENISE N. MORGAN
MARYANN MRAZ
NANCY D. PADAK
TIMOTHY RASINSKI

THE GUILFORD PRESS
New York   London

© 2009 The Guilford Press
A Division of Guilford Publications, Inc.
72 Spring Street, New York, NY 10012
www.guilford.com

Printed in the United States of America

This book is printed on acid-free paper.

Last digit is print number: 9 8 7 6 5 4 3 2 1

Library of Congress Cataloging-in-Publication Data

Independent reading : practical strategies for grades K–3 / Denise N. Morgan . . . [et al.].
    p. cm. — (Solving problems in the teaching of literacy)
  Includes bibliographical references and index.
  ISBN 978-1-60623-026-8 (hardcover : alk. paper)
  ISBN 978-1-60623-025-1 (pbk. : alk. paper)
1. Reading (Primary).   2. Children—Books and reading.   3. Reading—Parent participation.   I. Morgan, Denise N.
  LB1525.I45   2009
  372.4—dc22

                                                                          2008040907

To all those who fostered our love of reading

More specifically . . .

To my mother and father, Barbara and Graham Morgan,
who served as living examples of what it means to be readers.
Thank you for taking me to the library and for always buying
me books. Thanks also to my younger sister, Natalie W. Morgan,
who "agreed" to be my first student and listened
to my many read-alouds.

—D. N. M.

To my mom, Marilyn, and my dad, Steve, for reading all those
favorite books and nursery rhymes to me over and over
again, and for cheering on my literacy adventures to this very day.

—M.M.

To my mom, Ruth Collins, and the children's
librarians at Gale Borden Public Library in Elgin, Illinois.

—N. D. P.

To my mother and father—Laura and Chester Rasinski.
And also to George M. Cohan, Cole Porter, Irving Berlin,
Ira Gershwin, and the many other songwriters who helped
me see that wonderful words could be put to rhythm
and melody in song.

—T. R.

About the Authors

Denise N. Morgan, PhD, is Assistant Professor of Literacy Education at Kent State University in Kent, Ohio. She teaches and writes about reading and writing instruction, professional development, and literacy coaching. Dr. Morgan is an eclectic reader and an avid visitor to the library. She is enchanted with the writing of author Alice Hoffman and with the "Twilight" series by Stephenie Meyer. She keeps a small notebook with her at all times to record new titles she wants to read.

Maryann Mraz, PhD, is Associate Professor in the Department of Reading and Elementary Education at the University of North Carolina at Charlotte. She is the author of numerous books, articles, chapters, and instructional materials related to literacy education. Dr. Mraz's professional interests include literacy coaching, the professional development of teachers, and content-area literacy. She most enjoys reading memoirs, biographies, and travel books, and counts Connie Schultz, Elizabeth Gilbert, and Peter Mayle among her favorite authors.

Nancy D. Padak, EdD, is Distinguished Professor of Education at Kent State University, where she directs the Reading and Writing Center and works with the Ohio Literacy Resource Center. She has written and coauthored numerous books and articles related to literacy education. A former coeditor of *The Reading Teacher* and the *Journal of Literacy Research*, Dr. Padak is also a past president of the College Reading Association. Although she once read novels almost exclusively, she now enjoys the occasional biography or memoir. Among her favorite series books are the "Mapp and Lucia" books (E. F. Benson), "Miss Julia" books (Ann B. Ross), and "Big Stone Gap" books (Adriana Trigiani).

Timothy Rasinski, PhD, is Professor of Curriculum and Instruction at Kent State University, where he also helps direct the university's award-winning reading clinic for struggling readers. He has written and edited numerous books and professional articles on reading education. Dr. Rasinski has served as coeditor of *The Reading Teacher* and the *Journal of Literacy Research*. A past president of the College Reading Association, he recently served a term on the board of directors of the International Reading Association. He loves reading books on American history; his current favorite authors are David McCullough, Doris Kearns Goodwin, and Stephen Ambrose.

Preface

We are avid readers. To us, time spent reading is pure joy. As educators, there is much we want and need our students to do as readers. But in the end, what tops the list for many educators is that their students become lifelong readers, who read for information and pleasure.

As former classroom teachers, we have written this book as a way to help interested teachers, administrators, reading specialists, curriculum specialists, interventionists, and other concerned educators find ways to support independent reading in the K–3 classroom. Instructional time is limited—some might say woefully short—for all that you need to accomplish with students on a day-to-day basis. We have tried to share our best suggestions and tips based on reading research as a way to help you build and further support your foundation for independent reading.

We know there are many reasons why you are reading this book, and we offer the following suggestions:

- *If you are new to independent reading*, you might want to read the book from beginning to end. It might be helpful to form a small book group with other interested colleagues. You can read one chapter at a time and then create a plan of action based on the ideas presented in the chapter. For instance, after reading Chapter 5 on creating classroom libraries, you might take an inventory of your own library to see the kinds of books you already have (but might not be accessible) and to think about the kinds of books you would like to own. You might also think about gathering book reviews and booklists that might help guide your future purchases. Taking little actions after reading each chapter can support your desire to implement independent reading in your classroom.

- *If you want to refine your independent reading instruction*, you may choose to turn first to those chapters that match the areas of highest need or interest. Although our main ideas are referenced in each chapter and Chapters 2 and 3 are closely related, each chapter stands alone. It might be helpful to read this book with a colleague or group of colleagues. There is power and comfort in discussion, especially when addressing the nuances of reading instruction.

• *If you are familiar with independent reading but are teaching at a different grade level*, you might find the book helpful as a refresher or as a way to look at independent reading with an eye toward your new grade level. Revisiting the hows and whys of independent reading might be helpful as you consider the needs and abilities of your new students.

• *If you are not a classroom teacher*, you may have many different reasons for reading this book. As a principal, you may use this book for an overview of independent reading and as a springboard for beginning conversations with your teachers about including more time for students' independent daily reading. If you are a curriculum specialist, resource person, or interventionist, you might read the book for ideas that will enhance your work with small groups and individual children.

A LAST THOUGHT

Everything worthwhile takes time. Implementing independent reading will not happen overnight. It is a process of finding out what's exactly right for you and your students. Our book offers many strategies, ideas, suggestions, and forms to use as a starting point for forming your own group of passionate readers. It is our sincere hope that this book helps you to create a regular space for your students' independent reading and to create students who love to read. Happy reading.

DENISE N. MORGAN
MARYANN MRAZ
NANCY D. PADAK
TIMOTHY RASINSKI

Contents

INDEPENDENT READING

CHAPTER 1

Introduction

Learning to Read by Reading

MAKING A CRITICAL DECISION

On the first day of school, we teachers have to make a critical decision, one that shapes the year to come: Do we choose to see our students, regardless of age, as readers and writers?

We do. We believe children are readers the moment they make meaning from any kind of text. We don't define reading as the moment when a child gives a word-by-word accurate match with text. We believe children are reading the minute they recognize and can select their favorite book from the bookshelf, when they see the milk carton and say "milk" or when they yell the name of the restaurant, candy, book, or toy they happen to see at that time. We all know children who if asked to select a certain brand of cereal from a selection of other brands can find the correct box. We know children who can select their name from a group of other names or tell a story by looking at an illustration. We honor all these acts as reading.

We like to think in terms of what children can do rather than what they can't do. We believe children are readers even if they cannot yet read a single word on the page. We know that children might be able to "read" pictures, and so we give them books with rich illustrations. We know that they might be able to read books with simple captions, and so we provide those for them as well. We teach students and provide them with multiple demonstrations so they learn about book handling skills and the direction of print. In so doing, their knowledge of what to do while reading expands. To us, the most important thing is that students identify themselves as readers. And we think it is important that they view themselves as readers from their first moment in a classroom rather than waiting for some mythical time to become a "reader."

If on the first day of school, you tell your kindergarten and first-grade students that they are all readers, some students may look surprised. You might witness the "who me?" look on their faces. The easiest way to help students see themselves as readers is to show them immediately that they can read. You can, for example, have the students' names on sentence strips, index cards, or a name chart and, while pointing to each child's name, ask that child to read this word. By first choosing the children who are jumping out of their seats with eagerness, those students who are shy or are less familiar with their name will understand the pattern and say their name when it is their turn. And the smiles on their faces tell us the power of calling them readers from the first day onward.

You might also create an environmental print book of various objects the children know, including pictures of objects such as fruits and vegetables with the printed name underneath. The book might also include labels, ads, or logos from cereal boxes, snack foods, sports teams, well-known restaurants, and local areas of interest to the children. Each day, you might read this book with your students, celebrating their ability to read so many words. These are just a few of the many different ways to convey to students the message that they are readers.

The situation may be similar for second- and third-grade students. Some may enter your classroom with the perception that they are poor or weak readers. They may also have a surprised reaction when you identify all of your students as capable readers on that first day of school. Self-perceptions matter in learning. Your perceptions of students and expectations for their success matter as well. We must quickly identify those students who do not see themselves as readers and then work diligently to help them to develop a self-efficacy for reading.

We share this with you because this belief permeates our book. In both our earlier work as elementary school teachers and in our current work as university literacy professors and literacy consultants with numerous school districts and with the Kent State University Reading Clinic, we have worked with students whose literacy levels ranged from struggling to gifted. We acknowledge students will be reading in their own way, but we believe they are reading. We do not believe kids need preparation before they get books in their hands. So, we ask you to keep this in mind as you read this book. We know that students will do what they can when it is time for them to read books. As they know more about reading, they will do more with their books during this time. This belief guides the work we do with children and this belief supports the ideas we share with you throughout this book.

INDEPENDENT READING: WHY DOES IT MATTER?

When a child engages in independent reading, the child is able to have some degree of choice about what he or she reads. Independent reading can occur in both the home environment as well as in school. It can involve both oral and silent reading, and can encompass the use of a variety of reading materials such as poetry, scripts, stories, and songs. Key features of independent reading include the following:

- Children participate in the selection of the books and materials they read.
- Children are held responsible for their reading.
- Children are provided with a regular time period for independent reading, ideally on a daily basis.
- Children are provided with opportunities to share their insights of their own independent reading and to respond to the insights of others.

Researchers have made a compelling case for the positive impact of independent reading on the students' literacy skill development and their overall reading achievement: Children who read more increase their knowledge across literacy domains (Echols, West, Stanovich, & Zehr, 1996). Nagy and Anderson (1984) estimated that, by the time he or she reached middle school, the number of words read by an avid reader would approach 10,000,000 compared to 100,000 words read by a less motivated reader.

Additionally, studies have demonstrated that the benefits of independent reading exist, not only for already proficient readers, but also for readers across varying levels of achievement. "Even the child with limited reading and comprehension skills will build vocabulary and cognitive structures through reading" (Cunningham & Stanovich, 1998, p. 14). The more students read, the betters readers they become. Students who engage in wide, independent reading demonstrate gains in several key areas of literacy development. Those areas, summarized in Figure 1.1, include word recognition and vocabulary growth, language syntax, comprehension, and engagement and motivation. In the following sections, we highlight key research findings that connect independent reading to each of these components.

Word Recognition and Vocabulary Growth

Stanovich and West (1989) conducted one of the first studies that examined the connection between the amount of independent reading in which students engaged and their acquisition of automatic word

---

- Word recognition and vocabulary growth (e.g., Cunningham & Stanovich, 1998; Stanovich & West, 1989)

- Language syntax (e.g., Durkin, 1966; Hendrick & Cunningham, 2002)

- Comprehension (e.g., Anderson, Wilson, & Fielding, 1988; Krashen, 2004a)

- Engagement and motivation (e.g., Alvermann & Guthrie, 1993; Kragler, 2000; Mathewson, 1994)

FIGURE 1.1. Aspects of literacy learning that benefit from students' engagement in independent reading.

recognition. They found that more time spent engaged in independent reading was associated with better word recognition.

Share (1995) further explained that proficient readers develop automatic sight vocabularies with thousands of words, yet only a fraction of those words are formally taught in school. Familiarity with many sight words, then, is facilitated informally through engagement with text.

In terms of children's vocabulary development, similar findings were reported by Cullinan (2000): Independent reading helped to improve students' vocabulary growth as well as their spelling and grammar. Researchers generally agree that the amount of reading in which children are engaged is a primary contributor to individual differences in children's vocabulary knowledge (Cunningham & Stanovich, 1998).

Language Syntax

Durkin (1966) was one of the early researchers to point out that children acquire knowledge of written story structure, not so much through oral language use, but through actual reading experiences that involve the use of printed text. Hendrick and Cunningham (2002) reiterated that experiences with written language are needed in order for students to develop facility with language syntax as well as an understanding of text structure. Independent reading experiences provide opportunities for students to develop knowledge of language syntax.

Comprehension

Krashen (1993) found that children who engaged in independent reading in class, or who read more than their peers, performed as well or better on comprehension assessments than did their peers who spent less time reading or who didn't read at all. Similarly, Anderson, Wilson, and Fielding (1988) found that the number of books students read was the best predictor of achievement in reading comprehension, reading speed, and vocabulary knowledge.

Engagement and Motivation

The old saying "The person who knows how to read, but chooses not to, has little advantage over the person who can't read" sums up the problem of aliteracy—when students know how to read but choose not to do so. Most teachers strive to establish a learning environment that will not only teach children how to read, but that will provide them with intrinsic incentives to engage in reading, even when reading selections are not formally assigned. Teachers may, for example, seek to persuade students that different genres, topics, and authors are worth reading (Mathewson, 1994). Gambrell, Palmer, Codling, and Mazzoni (1996) describe highly motivated readers as self-determining; they are readers who want to read and choose to read for a wide range of reasons including curiosity, social interaction, and emotional satisfaction.

Independent reading is an important attribute of engaged reading (Alvermann & Guthrie, 1993). When student interest and student choice are integral parts of independent reading, student engagement in reading increases (Rasinski, 1988). Self-selection of reading materials provides students with opportunities to make decisions about their own reading, such as the types of materials they choose to read. Self-selected reading provides students with both authentic purposes for reading and opportunities to develop ownership of the reading process (Kragler, 2000).

If we wish to instill in children an enjoyment of reading that extends beyond assigned reading materials, then the importance of independent reading, and the self-selection process that is part of independent reading, must be recognized by educators, family members, and policy makers alike (Boulware & Foley, 1998). Furthermore, the expectancy–value theory of motivation (Eccles, 1983) purports that an individual's motivation to engage in a task is influenced by his or her expectation of success or failure (Paris & Oka, 1986). Students who have developed a self-efficacy for reading—who believe that they are capable and competent readers—are more likely to approach reading with the expectation of success and, in turn, they are more likely to achieve success in reading than students who do not expect to succeed.

IF INDEPENDENT READING IS SO IMPORTANT, WHY ISN'T EVERYBODY DOING IT?

While spending time curled up with a favorite book sounds delightful in theory, putting independent reading into practice, both in school and outside of school, can be challenging for several reasons. Time, for example, is often in short supply, so making time to read can be a challenge for some. In recent years, other issues have been found to affect independent reading in schools and in the home. Those issues include policy decisions, varying approaches to the implementation of independent reading in classrooms, and access to reading resources. The following section of this chapter will address each of these topics.

Policy Decisions

The passage of the No Child Left Behind Act of 2001 (2002), including the Reading First and Early Reading First programs, has intensified the attention focused on accountability and achievement in literacy education (Mraz & Rasinski, 2007). In Reading First and Early Reading First schools in particular, an increased emphasis on time spent in preparation for high-stakes assessments and the use of scripted core reading programs makes the preservation of independent reading time (and self-selected reading time) difficult for teachers to achieve.

In an effort to synthesize research-based knowledge about the effectiveness of various approaches to the teaching of reading, the National Reading Panel (National Institute of Child Health and Human Development, 2000a) examined experimental and quasi-experimental research related to reading and achievement. From their synthesis of those studies, the Panel identified five core components as key in learning to read: phonemic awareness, phonics or word decoding, reading fluency, vocabulary or word meaning, and comprehension. In its report, the National Reading Panel also raised questions about a so-called lack of evidence-based support for sustained silent reading, or independent reading time, in classrooms.

Based on the studies it reviewed, the Panel concluded that there was no empirical evidence to indicate that independent reading was associated with student success in reading. While the Panel acknowledged that there was correlational evidence showing that students who read more had higher levels of reading achievement, the Panel concluded that there was no experimental evidence showing how the amount of time students spend reading affects their reading achievement. This conclusion implied that independent reading should not be part of formal school reading programs. Many researchers took issue with the Panel's conclusion, pointing out that, based on the limited evidence it reviewed, the Panel could neither confirm nor deny that increasing the amount of time engaged in independent reading increases reading achievement (Cramer & Castle, 1994). Krashen (2004b) pointed out that the Panel had reviewed only 10 studies of sustained silent reading and, he contended, misinterpreted the findings of some of those. Despite concerns such as these, the Panel's conclusion that the benefits of independent reading are unsubstantiated has made it difficult for some educators to preserve independent reading time in their schools.

Subsequent studies have sought to use experimental and quasi-experimental methods to investigate the relationship between independent reading and reading achievement. For example, Samuels and Wu (2007) examined how the amount of time students spent engaged in independent reading influenced reading outcomes such as vocabulary, comprehension, and reading rate. They found that the amount of time students spent engaged in reading had a positive impact on all three of those outcomes. Lewis (2002) also explored the relationship between time spent reading and reading outcomes. Those findings indicated that students who spent time engaged in in-school independent reading scored higher on measures of reading achievement than did their peers who were not provided with independent reading time.

The conclusions drawn by the National Reading Panel based upon its review of select studies seems to have renewed the interest of many educators and researchers in the role of independent reading in learning to read. Findings from studies, such as those mentioned here, support the use of independent reading as one important component in developing readers who are both proficient and engaged.

Varying Approaches to Independent Reading in Classrooms

Traditional approaches to self-selected, independent reading in classrooms, sometimes called sustained silent reading (SSR) or Drop Everything and Read (DEAR), provide students with a consistent and fixed period of time to read self-selected materials silently. While students read their self-selected materials, the teacher serves as a model by reading his or her own reading material during each independent reading session. The goal of this routine is to provide students with opportunities to read and with models of engaged reading (Allington, 1977).

In contemporary approaches to self-selected reading in classrooms (e.g., Calkins, 2001; Fisher, 1995; Routman, 2003; Taberski, 2001), the role of the teacher is different. In these approaches to self-selected reading, while the students are engaged in reading, the teacher conferences with students and facilitates discussion of their reading experiences. For example, in Cunningham, Hall, and Sigmon's (1999) Four Blocks model, self-selected reading consists of several different segments. In the first segment (5–10 minutes), the teacher may read aloud to the students or introduce new topics or authors. A mini-lesson is often included in this segment. In the second segment (15–20 minutes) students read independently while the teacher conducts individual conferences with some of them. While the teacher does not confer with each student on a daily basis, he or she meets with each student about once each week. In the third and final segment of self-selected reading (5–10 minutes) one or two students share what they have read and classmates are invited to ask questions or engage in a discussion about the reading.

Comparative studies of traditional and contemporary models of self-selected reading suggest that students who discuss their reading with their teacher and peers benefit more from self-selected reading than students who simply read on their own without any follow-up or interaction (Manning & Manning, 1984). When self-selected reading is instructional in nature, teachers can guide students to texts that are appropriate for each student's interests and reading level. Teachers can also incorporate strategy instruction into self-selected reading time to support the development of comprehension and dis-

cussion skills (Gambrell, 2007). Details on ways to effectively implement independent reading time in school are addressed in Chapters
2 and 3.

Access to Reading Resources

Access to reading materials has been consistently identified as a vital
element in enhancing the reading development of children. All too
often, however, low-performing readers and children from lower
socioeconomic backgrounds are offered few opportunities beyond
the classroom to improve their reading proficiency (Coats & Taylor-
Clark, 2001). Children from low-income households typically have a
limited selection of books to read both within their homes and their
communities (McQuillan, 1998). In one study, for example, wealthier
communities were found to have up to three businesses selling children's books for every one such business that existed in poorer communities (Neuman & Celano, 2001).

Additionally, children who live in lower-socioeconomic-status
families typically have limited access to oral language interactions.
For example, the National Center for Family Literacy (2002) found
that, by age 4, children who live in poverty will have heard 32 million fewer words than children living in more affluent families (Hart
& Risley, 2003).

Access to reading materials in school is also important. In their
meta-analysis of studies that examined the relationship between
school resources and student achievement, Greenwald, Hedges, and
Laine (1996) found that the availability of a broad range of resources
was positively related to student achievement. Their findings suggest
that even moderate investments in reading resources may yield significant increases in student achievement.

Children who are offered opportunities to engage in independent, self-selected reading, and who have access to a variety of reading materials both in their classrooms and in their home and communities, read more widely and more often (International Reading
Association, 2000). These students, in turn, show greater gains in
reading achievement.

WHAT CAN BE DONE
TO IMPROVE INDEPENDENT
READING PRACTICES?

In the chapters that follow, we provide suggestions and resources for effectively implementing independent reading practices both in and outside of classrooms. In Chapter 2, "Independent Reading in Schools," we offer guidelines and suggestions for implementing independent reading programs in classrooms. Topics addressed include:

- Joining the literacy club: supporting reading and fostering readers
- Mini-lessons
- Managing independent reading time
- Engaging students in discussions about reading
- Identifying short-term goals
  - Finding time during a busy school day
  - Getting started
- Conferring with readers
- Sharing your reading life
- Helping students find the right book
- Book talks

Chapter 3, "Managing Independent Reading Programs," looks closely at ways to keep records of what has occurred during independent reading time. The following record-keeping templates are provided:

- Class Conference Summary Sheet
- Individual Conference Sheet
- Future Mini-Lessons
- Student Follow-Up Sheet
- Reading Logs
- Stop Reading Form
- Status of the Class Form
- Books I Want to Read

Chapter 4, "Ways to Read," examines options for independent reading routines and offers guidelines for in-school independent reading. Topics include:

- Readers' workshop
- Literature circles
  - Getting organized
  - Literature circle roles
  - Evaluating literature circles
  - Addressing dysfunctional groups
- Paired reading
- Buddy reading
- Tape-recorded reading
- Sustained silent reading

Chapter 5, "Creating Classroom Libraries," gives recommendations for selection, access, and readability issues, and includes a five-step process for evaluating the resources available in your classroom. The chapter includes lists of websites for learning about children's literature and starter lists of concept books, predictable literature, series books, and poetry books. Teachers are encouraged to consider the following questions as they build their own classroom library:

- How many books should we have in our classroom library?
- What kinds of books should we have in our classroom library?
- How can I find good books to add to the classroom library?
- How can I afford to purchase these books?
- What should our classroom library look like?

Chapter 6, "Independent Reading and Students with Special Issues," supports the belief that authentic independent reading can have a dramatic impact on struggling readers' academic achievement and attitude toward reading. We examine the major components of a reading program—phonemic awareness, phonics, vocabulary, fluency, and comprehension—and the connection of independent reading to each of these components.

In Chapter 7, "Assessment and Monitoring Issues in Independent Reading," we consider how teachers can use authentic reading experiences to identify areas of strength and weakness in students' reading, measure students' progress over time, and match materials to students' reading levels. Assessment tools, such as a multidimensional fluency rubric and a comprehension retelling rubric are provided. Topics addressed in this chapter include:

- Assessing reading interests
- Monitoring independent reading
- Assessing growth over time and proficiency in various elements of reading
  - Word recognition
  - Reading fluency–automaticity
  - Reading fluency–prosody
  - Vocabulary
  - Comprehension
  - Comprehension retelling

Finally, Chapter 8, "Family Literacy: Reading Together at Home," looks at the importance of parental involvement in children's literacy education. It examines why home literacy is important and suggests ways to develop an effective home literacy environment by reading aloud with children, building a spoken and listening vocabulary, and storytelling. School support of home literacy, particularly during the summer months, is also addressed. Resources include:

- A list of concepts of print
- Children's songs for rhyming
- Games that support reading
- Books and book sources for shared reading
- Ideas for supporting reading through dramatization
- Summer literacy activity suggestions
- A family reading survey

In addition, we have provided a professional development resource with questions appropriate for individual and group reflection to help you make the most of independent reading instruction in your classroom and school (see Appendix). It is our hope that this book will provide educators with valuable instructional and organizational tools as they seek to establish or refine the independent reading programs within their school communities.

CHAPTER 2

Independent Reading in Schools

Imagine reading this notice in your local paper:

> SIGN UP FOR SWIMMING LESSONS: SWIMSUITS UNNECESSARY
>
> We will teach your child how to swim without ever getting in the water. We will meet Monday–Friday for 1 hour. During that time, your child will learn all she or he needs to know about swimming without ever getting wet. We do this by practicing our different arm strokes in the air, holding our breath while sitting in chairs, and learning how to kick by lying on short tables.

Interested? Probably not. Even if you have a fear of water, you realize that these experiences will not help your child learn to swim. It is only by being in the water that children can integrate all they know about swimming to actually swim. Children get better at swimming by swimming. This is not unusual or unique. Most people learn how to do something or get better at doing something by engaging in that very act. The same idea applies to reading.

Readers get better at reading by reading. (But, we don't want kids just to get better at reading, we want them to love reading, embrace it, cherish it, see themselves as readers—but more about that later.) This is just as true for our youngest students as it is for a college professor. The very act of getting better at reading requires that a person have regular time to read. Our teaching day is so full. We read aloud to children so that they are immersed in wondrous words, lovely language, and delightful tales/experiences from all genres. We invite them to join in on the joyous time of reading together during shared reading, provide students with small group tailored instruction during guided reading, and support them in feverishly discussing books during literature study. Students learn about all aspects of reading when we engage with them in the meaningful, authentic experiences mentioned above. However, they also need time to simply practice their reading, and that is where the powerful practice of independent reading takes center stage.

Part of our instructional day should be devoted to students reading independently. This time offers students the valuable practice we know all learners need. Independent reading allows students to have the time to apply all they know about reading to books of their choosing.

JOINING THE CLUB/SUPPORTING READERS/ FOSTERING READERS

We need students to realize they are full-fledged members of the literacy club (Smith, 1988), a group of people who find value and meaning in reading and writing. Many students come to school already members of the literacy club while some do not. Whatever the case, our job as teachers is to ensure that all students know they are welcome and capable of joining this club, this group of people who appreciate reading and writing and are confident that their earliest attempts to read and write are appreciated and respected. Being members of the literacy club helps students see themselves as readers and writers and understand that these acts are not just something that "other people do." It is important that students view themselves as people who choose to read, people who know what they want to read next, and people who could not imagine a life without books and reading. We want to help students develop a hunger for books (Fox, 2001) and deepen their view of themselves as readers (Mooney, 1990). Part of our responsibility is to ensure that reading and writing are accessible to students while fostering a low- to no-risk environment for students as they engage in these complex literacy tasks. We want to create students who can and do read (Allington, 2006), students who read for the joy and delight of reading (Atwell, 2007). One way to support this low-risk environment is to find daily time for independent reading, time when students make choices about what they will read.

THE ELEGANCE OF A PREDICTABLE STRUCTURE

Independent reading offers students three opportunities:

1. Time to learn something specific about reading (mini-lesson)
2. Time to read
3. Time to talk about their reading (sharing) (see Figure 2.1)

This predictable structure provides balance for students. Each day they know they will learn about some aspect of reading through a short 5- to 15-minute mini-lesson, have ample time to read, and then time to talk about their reading with a partner or with the whole class. Students know what to expect within this structure. Instead of wondering if they will get time to read each day, students can focus on what they will read or can anticipate what will happen next in their books. This simple structure ensures that each day students learn something about reading, read in class, and then talk about their reading, which helps them understand that part of their

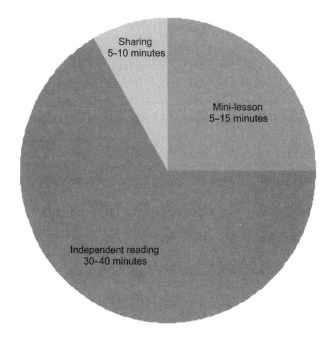

FIGURE 2.1. Reading workshop.

responsibility as readers is to be able to say something about their books to another person. This sends the message that talking about books is important. There is nothing more disheartening when a student finishes a book and can only shrug his or her shoulders when asked about the book, so this talk time after reading is crucial.

MINI-LESSONS: TIME TO LEARN
SOMETHING SPECIFIC ABOUT READING

Mini-lessons can best be thought of as powerful teaching moments. Each mini-lesson should teach the students something about reading. These short, focused lessons are designed to pack a punch quickly so as not to interfere with reading time. Mini-lessons can run anywhere from 5 to 15 minutes depending on the topic being addressed.

To prepare for the mini-lesson the teacher selects a topic, most often something she or he sees the students need and finds a clear, memorable example to help the students understand this concept. The idea can be revisited over time so there is less pressure to try and "get it all in." In fact, with mini-lessons the opposite is true. You want to declutter your potential lesson until you determine its essence. The essence of the lesson could deal with some aspect that helps students better understand how books work (mini-lessons about literary aspects), what occurs in a reader's head while reading (mini-lessons about reading processes), or how to work within the guidelines for reading workshop (mini-lessons about procedures). One way to help streamline your teaching during mini-lessons is to summarize it in one sentence. This helps identify the most important idea or aspect to teach to help keep your lessons brief. If you are concerned about this short teaching time, remember, independent reading is just one part of a balanced literacy program. You are teaching through reading aloud, sharing reading, guided reading, and literature study. Independent reading is just one experience for fostering readers' development.

All mini-lessons should help students understand how and why they might use this information in their own reading. It is easy to teach a lesson and fail to explicitly mention how this can help students. Failure to do so can sometimes make the lesson seem like a floating piece of knowledge, a piece of information not connected to something bigger. Naming this connection for the students helps them anchor this new knowledge. You might say:

> "The reason why it can be helpful to make connections when we read is so that we can draw upon our experiences to help us better understand the book. Sometimes if we have been in a similar situation or place we know to possibly expect certain things to happen. This knowledge can help you better use what you know to become more involved with the book."

Or:

> "It is important that you look for little signs along the way of your main character changing. It is rare for a character not to change in some way from the beginning of the book to the end of the book. You need to be on the lookout for those little and, sometimes, big signs of change throughout the book because that helps you understand the evolution of the main character."

In essence, what you are trying to do in mini-lessons is teach the students something that will be added to their knowledge about books and reading. What you teach depends directly on what your students need to know to move forward as readers. Part of what you teach will be from your direct observations and assessments of the students as readers along with your district and state standards. Mini-lessons are a way to teach students something about reading while preserving enough time for students to read independently. A starter list of mini-lesson topics is provided in Figure 2.2.

TIME TO READ

Time to read is the heart of independent reading. All of our wonderful teaching will not matter if we do not protect time for students to read books of their choosing and apply what they have learned about reading in books that are just right for them. Protecting this time is critical. It should become the brushing-your-teeth-before-bed nonnegotiable of the school day. You must determine how long you want your students to read each day. Of course, you will have to build up

- Reading is about meaning
- Why readers reread books
- How to keep track of books read
- How to check out books from the classroom library
- How to choose a book to read
- What to do if you are finished reading
- Where to find book reviews
- Looking for letters and words that you know
- Why some books are easy, hard, or just right
- When to abandon a book
- Introducing students to different genres they may wish to read
- The joy of finding an author you love
- How to find books you may want to read next
- How series books work
- What to do when you come to a word you don't know
  - Look at the picture
  - Think about what would make sense
  - Think about what would make sense and look at the first letter of the word
  - Think about what would make sense and look at the last letter of a word
  - Look for part of a word that you know
  - Go back to the beginning of the sentence and begin again and think about what would make sense
  - Read to the end of the sentence and then come back and begin the sentence again
  - When to ask to for help

FIGURE 2.2. Mini-lesson possibilities.

to this time. Just as if you were new to running, you most likely would not run for 40 minutes the first time you laced up your sneakers. You would build up your stamina over time. Stamina for reading is one of the most important "muscles" students can develop. You need stamina to read for any length of time. You need stamina to read the new *Harry Potter* book. You need stamina to read passage after passage on the state reading test. Good readers have stamina. It isn't so much considered stamina when we are older, just good fortune to be able to say you spend all day Saturday beginning and finishing a 400-page book because you didn't want to stop. Ask any *Harry Potter* fans for their story about reading the last book. Most people will proudly tell you when they finished the book ("I got it Friday at midnight and I was finished by Saturday morning at 10," or "It only took me 2 days to finish"). These readers have stamina.

You can support students in building stamina for reading by beginning with small amounts of time and adding more minutes along the way. In the first few days of independent reading you might simply set a timer for 8 to 10 minutes. You want the time to be short enough so that all students are engaged and a bit disappointed when the timer sounds. The best sound you can hear is a collective sigh of "ahhh" to signal their disappointment that independent reading time is over. During their reading time, it will be helpful to just observe your students and notice:

- Who gets started right away?
- Who has a difficult time finding a book and getting settled?
- Who keeps switching books, never quite finishing one before beginning another?
- Who gets lost in a book?
- Who seems easily distracted?

All of this information tells you something about your students but also provides you with some direction for future mini-lessons. For example, if you see that several students are not entering the reading zone (Atwell, 2007), that state where they are enthralled with and engrossed in their books, you could talk to the students about what it feels like to enter the reading zone, where all you are thinking about is the story and everything else melts away. Fellow classmates can describe their feelings during this time so that other students who may not have fully encountered this feeling previously can now look for times when they feel this way. Sharing this information with students informs them about the possibility of this wonderful feeling of getting lost in a book, describing it in such a way that when they experience it, they know have entered their own reading zone.

Gradually, add minutes to the timer, moving up by amounts you deem appropriate. Some teachers forgo the timer and write the ending time for independent reading on the board so that all students know when they are expected to move to sharing. You may want to give your students a 2-minute warning before they are expected to stop reading. This way they can try and finish that sentence or paragraph before sharing. If they can help it, readers do not stop reading mid-sentence; most choose an appropriate stopping point. You can tell your students, "Two more minutes. Please come to a good stopping point." When the time is up, the students know to transition to the meeting area for sharing. There might be a student or two who is quickly finishing up a paragraph or a page and does not come to the meeting area with the other students immediately, but we don't think that is such a bad thing.

SHARING TIME TO TALK ABOUT READING

While reading a great book, we often feel compelled to share with others. We might tell them, "You won't believe this book I am read-ing," or "I can't put this book down," or "You have to read this book when I am finished." It could also be that you are haunted by a book and must talk about your experience with a friend as a way to help you process a particular event or scene. As adults, we find time to talk about books because we have learned that it is a rewarding aspect of reading and very much a part of who we are. Therefore, we want to ensure that students have sharing time following their quiet reading time as a way to process their book, to allow a pleasant experience to linger, an excitement to grow, or a dissatisfaction to be named.

Sharing time allows students to have that same experience each day. The teacher invites students to come to the meeting area. It can be nice to ask students to sit in a circle so they can see one another easily. This is important for when you ask a particular question and want all students to share a response. Sharing time should reflect the needs of the group.

One day, you might ask students to reflect upon that day's mini-lesson and share examples that support or extend the idea brought forth in the day's discussion. For example, if the day's mini-lesson highlighted the different ways authors help readers understand how time passes in their books, you might ask students prior to begin-ning of their independent reading time to pay attention to how time moves throughout their book. Later, at sharing time, those students who found examples share them with the rest of the class. Students might confirm examples you shared with the class earlier, or they might identify new ways their authors noted time changes. This sharing enlarges all students' understanding. Another day during sharing time, you might ask students to speak with a conversation partner about their books, leaving it open for students to speak about whatever is foremost in their minds. Partners can be assigned or you can pair students as conversation buddies that change daily, weekly, or monthly. If the class has been studying how characters change, you could ask students to identify how they believe their main character has changed or if they are seeing signs of change yet. If the students are sitting in a circle, it will be very easy for students to quickly respond as you move clockwise. Responding in a circle requires that all students consider the question and think about their books in a specific way.

Sharing time is also teaching time. This time should not be considered fluff or unnecessary. You can gather formative assessment data on what students know about a particular topic. Students can learn from and with each other as they listen to each other's comments. You can gather additional examples for mini-lessons based on what students find in their reading. This time should be carefully scheduled as it is easy to "not get to sharing time" because of other obligations. By ensuring daily time for sharing, you send the message that talking and thinking about books is important and is what members of the literacy club do.

IDENTIFYING SHORT-TERM GOALS

Getting independent reading up and running is a process, one that simply takes time. As teachers, you set goals and develop a vision for where you want your students to be by the end of the year. June can feel far away when you are trying to establish a routine in September, so it is important that you also consider some short-term goals for independent reading to help you get started. These goals can help you focus and feel a sense of accomplishment while you still keep your eye on the big picture. Here are two possible short-term goals to consider:

- Getting kids to love and look forward to reading time
- Establishing a management system that seems doable

How do these feel to you? Do you have other goals that you would like to include or substitute? You may choose to pursue other short-term goals, but these are two that have helped teachers find focus during those beginning weeks of school.

When students see and experience their independent reading time as a treat or pleasure, they look forward to this time and hold us accountable for making sure they read daily. In the beginning, students will often ask "Will we get to read today?" but once they understand that they will read everyday, you soon may hear "I can't wait to read today." This reading time becomes like lunch, something we all appreciate and look forward to. Since students know with certainty that it will occur, they can anticipate this reading time. It is hard to look forward to or make plans for something that may or may not occur.

Another important goal to consider is how to manage the documentation of this independent reading time. If you are willing to devote ample time to daily reading, you need to be able to find a way to keep track of your conversations with and observations of your students. You have to find, design, or modify forms that will allow you to capture the kinds of notes and evidence that will inform your teaching and your knowledge of each student. You need to establish a routine that has the right fit for you. You might go through several iterations of forms to find one that works. (Several ideas for record keeping are shared in Chapter 3.) This is simply part of the process.

Short-term goals make establishing an independent reading time within your classroom seem possible. Students need time to understand the expectations for independent reading, as they do for any aspect of the school day. Identifying short-term goals provides a clear direction for your early work with students, and success can be seen relatively early on in the process. If you are brand new to establishing independent reading in your classroom, short-term goals can help you feel like you are taking successful small steps toward your larger goal.

FINDING TIME DURING A BUSY SCHOOL DAY

There are only so many hours in a school day, and only so much time can be devoted to literacy instruction. If you are not sure how you will find time for your students to independently read, consider conducting a time audit. For the next few days, scrutinize your schedule looking for lost or wasted moments of time that you can add to your literacy instruction. Examine how students are spending their time during literacy instruction and analyze the educational payoff they receive from doing a particular activity or engagement. There are two very important questions you can ask to help yourself make hard decisions:

- How much of what I am asking students to do is actual reading versus how much of what they are being asked to do is stuff about reading (but not actual reading)?
- How authentic is what my students are doing to what a reader does in the real world?

These questions may help you discover additional time. We know that there is no easy way to find time; rather, teachers hunt for or make time because they believe and know that independent reading time is crucial for students' development as readers.

THE FIRST DAY

Don't wait too long to begin independent reading. Many teachers feel that they need to make sure everything is in place first, teaching procedural mini-lessons, lessons designed to help students understand how the workshop will function, across several weeks to ensure that students are familiar with the expectations during this time. We encourage you to begin after a few introductory, get acquainted, or reacquainted with school days. On the first day you begin, all the students need to know is that for a set amount of time each day they will get to read a book(s) of their choosing. In the younger grades, you could place a basket or tub of books on the tables and allow the students to choose from those books to read. For older students, let them know they should bring in a book they want to read a day or two before you begin. Prior to beginning, you could talk about some of the books you have in your classroom library as a way to help alleviate the problem of "I don't know what to read" or not having a book on the first day you are ready to begin.

To introduce this new procedure you could begin simply by saying:

> "This year is going to be very exciting because each day we will have time to read books we want to read. There is a basket of books on each table. Today please read from these books during our independent reading time. I will set the timer for 10 minutes. Please keep reading during that time. If you finish a book, please find another one to read. Your job is to read softly or quietly so you do not disturb other readers. When 10 minutes are up, we will get together and talk about what you read. Any questions? Okay, happy reading."

Or if students brought their own books to read you might say:

> "I am so excited to see all of the interesting books you brought to read today. Each day we will have time to read so it will be your responsibility to make sure you have your book in class every day. Today I will set the timer for 10 minutes. You should be reading this entire time. It will be important that you read silently so you will not disturb other readers. When 10 minutes are up, we will get together and talk about what you read. Any questions? Okay, happy reading."

Quite simply, in the beginning, you want your students to quickly get used to spending a set amount of time reading. The goal is to simplify your expectations at first merely so that kids get started reading right away rather than waiting until all classroom rules and expectations have been addressed.

As you observe your students, it is likely that you will notice some issues that you would like to address promptly. That is normal and to be expected. These issues become things you *teach into*, meaning you identify those issues of your greatest concern and you teach your students how to do those things better or more smoothly. Any concern or issue today merely becomes tomorrow's mini-lesson.

CONFERRING WITH READERS

Conferring with your students reader to reader might become one of the most rewarding parts of your day. While the rest of the class is reading, you have an opportunity to meet one-on-one with a student to talk about books and to learn more about what the student is noticing and thinking about the book. During this time you learn more about your students as readers, gather evidence of what they already know how to do as readers, and determine what a particular student or the whole class needs to learn next. There are many important decisions to consider when thinking about structuring your conferences.

Determining Your Stance

The stance you decide to take when meeting with your students sets the tone for your conferences. We encourage you to consider the stance of a reader talking to another reader. This way, when you confer with students it becomes more about wanting to know how it is going for the student rather than a test to see whether he or she understood the book. Many teachers begin their conference by checking in with the student and asking, "How is it going for you?" and "What are you learning about yourself as a reader?" thus putting the focus on the student's experience in reading rather than asking for a retelling of the book.

As teachers, we have colleagues or superiors observe our teaching occasionally. There is a fundamental difference in how we feel if we know the person observing is checking on us to see if we are teaching a certain way or if the person is observing to see what we are currently doing as teachers. The first experience might bring anxiety for most, while the second feels a bit more comfortable. We believe students are no different. They intuitively know the difference between being tested to see if they really read the book and having a conversation about a book with another interested person. What stance will you take when you confer with children: tester or fellow reader? Figure

2.3 contains some additional questions you may wish to ask your students when conferring.

Taking Notes

It is critical that you capture your insights, questions, and surprises from your conferences. It is easy to forget the brilliant moments you have with your students in this one-on-one setting. When you are engrossed in the conference and then in a hurry to confer with the next child, it is easy to think you will write notes later on. But we know as teachers, later never brings us time to write those notes. It can help to have a clipboard that you carry around from conference to conference. There are many ways to take notes. You have to try and find the way that makes taking notes easiest for you. Some people use sticky notes and some use sticky labels that they later transfer to the child's page in an assessment notebook. Or you could simply gather the pages for the students you will confer with that day and write directly on those sheets.

What you take notes on depends on what information you want and need to gather about each child. You might want to record what students are noticing about themselves as readers. You might want to listen to the child read and capture the miscues so you can coach the child to think about his or her use of reading strategies afterwards. You might ask the students something specific about their book that is directly tied to day's mini-lesson. For example, a mini-lesson on

- How is your reading going?
- What is happening in the book so far that is interesting to you?
- Is there anything you need help with?
- Have you come across anything that was confusing to you today? If so, what did you do?
- How did you choose this book to read?
- What do you plan to read after this book?
- Since you have already read several books by this author, what can you expect to happen in this book?
- Have you noticed anything in your reading that connects to today's mini-lesson?
- What makes your main character interesting to you?
- What are you enjoying most about your book?

FIGURE 2.3. Questions to pose while conferring with students.

setting could help students understand that in some books, the setting is critical to the story. It matters that the book takes place in a particular part of the country, town, or even teacher's classroom because those settings offer particular conditions that influence the characters. At the same time, there are stories that have generic settings, say an apartment, a town, or an elementary school and in these cases the setting does not heavily influence the characters' actions. After talking about these ideas and using examples from read-alouds and other shared stories the students know, you could inform the students that in their conferences this week you would like to talk with them about the setting of their books. You will ask them to think about whether the setting plays an important or not so important role in their book and to provide evidence for why they came to that decision. When you confer with students that week, you can take particular note about their understanding of the role of setting in their story. You could take notes on their use of evidence (or lack of evidence) and even note if you feel their responses demonstrate high understanding (marked by a plus sign), good understanding (marked with a check), showed confusion (marked with a question mark) or poor understanding (marked with a minus sign). After collecting that information, you can decide whether the entire class would benefit from another mini-lesson about this topic, whether a small group needs to be pulled, or whether you need more one-on-one time with a particular child. Taking notes provides evidence of what the students know how to do and provides direction for where you might want to take the students as readers next.

Letting Students Know What to Expect during Conferences

Tell students why you are conferring with them and what to expect so they are not worried about meeting one-on-one with you. Students should understand the purpose and structure of these meetings. During your mini-lesson you could tell the students:

"I am going to start meeting with individual students today while everyone is independently reading. When I come visit you, we will talk about your reading. I want to know how your reading is going, what you think about your book, and other questions readers like to ask other readers. I might ask you to read a bit to me. While we are talking I will take notes about the smart things you say and I will make some reminder notes for myself. Our conferences won't last long, just a few minutes, and then I will meet with someone else. I won't be able to get to everyone today but I plan to see everyone by the end of the week. Any questions?"

By sharing this kind of information you are setting the tone for what students should expect to happen during this conferring time. Some teachers identify the students they will be conferring with each day so that students do not spend their reading time wondering, "Am I next?" Some teachers meet with certain students on certain days and create a list of the students they confer with on Monday, Tuesday, and so on. See Figure 2.4.

Side-by-Side Conferences

One type of reading conference to consider with our youngest readers is a side-by-side reading conference (Segel, 1990) in which you simply sit next to a child and share a book or two. You can read to the child, the child could read to you, or you can read the book together. What is important is that during this time you carefully watch what the child does, says, and notices during the reading. Side-by-side conferences are an opportunity to see what reading behaviors and concepts about print the child knows. This should be a joyous time where you get to know and learn about one child. It's a no-pressure situation.

Monday	Tuesday	Wednesday	Thursday	Friday
Gavin	Natalie	Will	Barb	Mary Margaret
Julie	Jodi	Jeff	Gayle	Kate
Pam	Barbara	Leslie	Joe	Sarah Jayne
Becca	Graham	Katlyn	Scott	Lucy
Patrick	Jessica	Charlotte	Max	Michael

FIGURE 2.4. Example of a daily conference schedule.

But by spending 10 minutes with one child and a book, you can learn a great deal about your students that will inform your earliest teaching.

THE IMPORTANCE OF TRUST

There is trust involved when students are allowed to read books of their choosing. There will be many times when the students are reading books you have not read. When you confer with students and really listen to what they say and how they talk about the book, you will be able to determine understanding. Sometimes teachers worry that kids could make things up about the book and they would not know. We acknowledge that this *could* happen, but we have found that is the exception rather than the rule. If you have this concern with a particular child, there are several things you can do.

- You could begin reading the same book as the child; sometimes just a few chapters will give you enough understanding to have a more in-depth conversation with the student.
- You could ask the student to choose from several books that you have already read so when you confer with the child you have a better sense of the child's understanding.
- You could ask the child to read a short story you think is well-matched to the child's reading ability and if the child is able to talk about the story with you then you can assume that the child can engage in the same kind of thinking on another book of similar difficulty.
- Ask the child to read aloud from his or her book. Sometimes you can clearly hear students make meaning through their oral reading. Their pauses, expressions, tone, and pace often demonstrate how they understand the text. Awkward phrasing and monotone reading may hint at a child's limited understanding of the text.
- You could pay particular attention to what the child does during guided reading. A child actively making meaning and using appropriate strategies while reading in a small group is most likely going to apply the same appropriate strategies while reading a book of her choosing.

Occasionally, you may wish to monitor a student or students closely in the beginning, but we have found that the number of students who will take this responsibility of trust seriously is exciting. We understand that it may be an initial leap of faith and trust to allow students to read books you haven't read, but we believe that sending the message that you trust your students is worth the risk.

SHARING YOUR READING LIFE

Never underestimate the power of sharing who you are as a reader with your students. Students respond to your enthusiasm and excitement about books and reading. It is easy to feel a connection with people when you know something about how they live their reading life. In Figure 2.5 we share several aspects of your reading life that you could share with your students, and we also share the kinds of things we might actually say to the students.

This talk is conversational, book fiend to book fiend or future

If you wanted to share …	It might sound like …
Why you read	"I read because I absolutely, positively love it. It brings me such joy. I read because it makes me smarter, provides me with different experiences, and allows me to get to know people that I might not otherwise ever encounter. But it is also because I really, really love it. I can't imagine my life without books."
When you read	"I tend to always bring a book with me so I am never bothered or upset if I get somewhere early or if someone I am waiting for is late. I will even take a book to the post office (there are always long lines). I was driving home one day and there was an accident and the cars were not moving, so I picked up my book and was able to read a few pages before we were able to move again."
Where you read	"I will read anywhere, but mainly I read in my bed and lying on my couch. I sometimes read at the kitchen table, but usually I prefer some place really comfortable. I read on my deck, on the couch (in the winter having a heating pad and blanket are important), in my bed (always, every night, no matter how tired I am). In beach chairs on vacation. Being comfy is important." *(continued)*

How you keep track of your books you have read or want to read	"I keep a small notebook in my purse so I can jot down the titles of books that I want to read. Sometimes I rip out the page from my magazine if my notebook is not close by. I often go to the library and request the titles in my notebook. I cross the title off when I finish reading the book. Right now I have about 40 titles in my notebook. I may not ever get to read them all, but I like having many titles to explore."
How you find books	"I trust my husband, Gary, on this. He spends all year looking for books for me and he really knows my taste. He gives me a box of books each year for my birthday and for Christmas. I also listen to friends and my sissy."
Where you keep your books	"Bookshelves! They are all over the family room of our house. We have a couple of bookshelves at the lake, too. My current book is always on a table beside my bed."
The pleasure of owning books and checking out books from the library	"I love going to the library. Before I move someplace new, I visit to find a place to live. While I am there, one thing I have to do is find the local library. It is important for me to see what the library looks like, see how it is organized, and how their check-out system works. It is important for me to know a little bit about the library I will be visiting frequently once I move to this new town. Now that I live here, I go to the library about once a week. I request books online so much that I even have my number memorized and it is 13 numbers long."
A book you are still thinking about	"*A Farewell to Arms* because my son, Matt, thinks it's the best novel ever written. So I'm thinking (a) is it? and (b) if it isn't, what is?"
Your personal beliefs about books	"Read whatever you want to; just read."
Your book gurus	"I have a friend Christy who gives the best book suggestions. I have liked almost every book she has ever recommended to me. She has recommended some of my favorite books."
Other book quirks	"I have a lot of bookmarks. I trade them off. No real system for this, but it's fun to do. I love standing in front of a bookshelf, developing a short list of titles, then thumbing through them to see which one I'll be reading next." "Sometimes it's worth it to read really good books again. I read *To Kill a Mockingbird*, for example, every few years. And I read *Fried Green Tomatoes* again not long ago."

FIGURE 2.5. Sharing your reading life.

book fiend. By sharing your reading life with your students, you help them envision what this life is like and what it might be for them. You will, without a doubt, have many students who already lead rich reading lives. There will be others who have not developed such an expansive identity of themselves as readers. Your sharing allows students to play with and imagine possibilities. Over the course of several days, it would be easy to share many aspects of your reading life from the list above with your students. Many students will also have stories to share about their reading lives, so provide time for their sharing also. To develop a community of readers, students will need to hear each other's stories. You will be surprised at how much your students and you will draw upon this information throughout the year.

MAKING A BOOK MATCH

One of the earliest mini-lessons you may teach will be designed to help each student find the right book. If students are going to spend precious class time each day reading, you will want to help them make good choices, choices in which they can get the most from their reading experience. Students get the most from reading texts that offer just a bit of reading challenge. Too much challenge usually means the student will have to work too hard reading. Too little challenge and the student may not be learning anything new from the current book. The balance comes in finding a just-right book, so that the student reads text that offers just a bit of challenge but not enough to consistently interrupt the child's understanding or cause difficulties. There is no precise formula for helping kids find their just-right books. Much of the match depends on interest and prior knowledge. A student who knows a great deal about dinosaurs might be able to read a more advanced book about this topic than a similarly written book about an unknown topic.

Whereas most reading experience should be in books that are just right for students, they should have the opportunity to occasionally read books that might be considered challenging or books that are considered easy or "beach" books. There is satisfaction in reading a challenging book as there is pleasure in reading easy "beach" books.

We want students spending most of their time reading just-right books along with a few challenging texts and easy texts for variety.

Many teachers use students' accuracy scores on informal reading inventories to select appropriate books. They often use the scale shown in Figure 2.6. Whereas using accuracy scores may help us as teachers guide students to an appropriate book, we want to help students learn how to determine for themselves if a book is just-right, challenging, or easy. Students need to understand the kind of inner conversation they should have when selecting a book.

Teachers can ask students to conduct the five-finger test when selecting a book. Students keep track on their fingers the number of words they have difficulty with on a page. If all five fingers are used before the student reaches the end of the page, the book may be too difficult, and the child should find another book. With older students, you may ask them to record the words they have difficulty with on paper so you can confer with them about the types of words missed. Once you have this information you can consider: Were the words missed mainly specialized vocabulary or unusual names? Did the reader have more trouble near the beginning of the book? In some cases, depending on the errors, a book still might

Identifying type of reading	% accuracy	When is this best for students?
Independent reading level	98–100%	This would be considered a just-right read during independent reading. The child is making few errors on this book, and thus most of his effort will be directed at making meaning rather than word solving.
Instructional reading level	93–97%	This kind of book is often appropriate for small group instruction as the students need a bit of help to ensure a good reading.
Frustration reading level	92% and below	This book is too often hard for the student. The student would have to work too hard. The reader would likely have difficulty understanding this book.

FIGURE 2.6. Accuracy levels.

be appropriate for the child. In both cases, it is important to look beyond the mere number of words to the kinds of words and concepts missed. There is never a hard and fast rule for selecting an appropriate book.

THE EXCITEMENT OF BOOK TALKS

There is nothing more exciting than learning about new wonderful books. One easy way to ensure that your students know about new books is to conduct regular book talks. Book talks can be considered short little teasers to "sell" books to children. These brief personal introductions to the books should whet children's appetites for books they "must" read.

Although there is no standard way to conduct a book talk, you will want to make sure they are much more than simple summaries. Here are some ideas to consider including when crafting your book talks:

- Title and author
- Genre
- Subject of book or plot summary
- Best feature of the book
- Interesting words that describe the book
- Who should read the book
- Keep it short, under 3 minutes

One of the most important goals for your book talks is to convey excitement and energy for the book, sharing a bit of "why you should read this" for the children. So the children end up thinking things like:

- "I love science fiction. I have not heard of that author. I can't wait to read her book."
- "I am going to read this book because I want to know what happens to that little girl."
- "Mrs. Cobb said this was the best book she has read in a long time. I want to read that."

- "I have not read a mystery before but three kids in the class said they loved this book and then all started laughing about a certain part. I want to read that book."
- "How can a mom not know her child's name? I have to read to find out what is wrong with that mom."
- "I read that other book by Cynthia Rylant and I don't know about this series. I want to try that book."

Book talks can take place during mini-lesson time. Book talks can help you accomplish many things in your classroom such as:

- *Introducing the classroom library.* This is helpful especially in the beginning of the year when the students don't know the books you have on your shelves.
- *Introducing newly purchased books.* When you bring new books into the classroom, you will want to familiarize students with new titles.
- *Introducing new books you have not read.* During a book talk a "reader" can give an opinion about a book (especially helpful with chapter books). Sometimes you can share why you purchased the book and then ask if someone would volunteer to read it and talk to you about it. This is a good way to get a reader's stamp of approval for a book.
- *Getting books into the children's hands.* A book-talked book never goes unnoticed or unread by the children. Often, there is a scramble for the book so consider devising a way to handle the interest. Margaret Nickerson, a second grade teacher, routinely gave book talks in her classroom. One book in particular was so popular that the students devised a sign-up sheet for the book and hung it on the wall. This way, readers knew their position and could anticipate when it was their turn to read the book.

Other important things to remember about book talks:

- Variety is key. Your students should not think there is one way to "do" a book talk. Cat Hamilton, a teacher, once sang before she talked about her book. That grabbed our attention. You want to allow enough flexibility that students feel "free" to use their imaginations and talents.

 • Book talks should carry the same excitement as when your best friend tells you about a book you must read.

 • Book talks are about helping children get "in the know" about books. Just as there are hot books that create a buzz with adults ("Have you read *The Glass Castle*? It is getting a lot of press and I hear it is fabulous"), there will be buzz books for children. They too will be able to nod their heads and say, "I've heard of it but have not read it yet" or "I've read it and it is great."

 • Book talks are a way to share books on a regular basis and create a literary buzz in your own classroom.

HAVE STUDENTS GIVE BOOK TALKS

Teach students how to do book talks. Students should be able to sign up as they decide they want to do a book talk to the class. Help children understanding the perimeters of book talks (short, to the point, you don't want to give too much away), and they will amaze you with what they will think to say or do with the book.

Students can also learn to write written recommendations about their books. Their books can be displayed in a special spot in the room (just like in the bookstores) so that others can see what their classmates are reading and determine if they want to read the book as well.

EVALUATING YOUR READING
TIME WITH STUDENTS

It is easy to have students assess their work during independent reading by examining their experience against a rubric you share or one that is jointly created. At the end of independent reading, ask students to assess the class against a rubric describing the conditions of workshop. You may come up with criteria for judging the time in categories such as "outstanding," "wow," "so-so," and "oops" (Calkins, 2001), use numbers, or even levels of smiley faces to evaluate the day. Regardless of what you choose, you may want students to consider issues such as focused attention while reading, movement, and noise level, along with additional criteria you and your students deem important. For example, the class might determine they have had an outstanding reading day when the following occurs:

- All students read quietly and were engaged in their reading.
- People stayed in their places; there was not distracting movement.
- Students thought about their reading and used reading strategies to help them when they had difficulty.
- It felt like it was a good reading day.

What makes the list is largely determined by what is important to you and your students and what your vision is for this independent reading time.

OUR ADVICE: DON'T WAIT

We are a society that appreciates new beginnings. January 1 is greeted with much anticipation. Not only is it the start of a new year but it is often the beginning of new resolutions. Many enjoy the idea of starting fresh in the new year so that even if people want to make a change in November, they often wait until January 1 to undertake said idea. This pattern happens in schools also. Often teachers choose to wait to implement an idea until a new school year, even if that idea occurs to them in November. If you happen to read this book while the school year is in session, our plea is to begin independent reading now. Don't wait. Children adjust to new schedules given clear explanations and reasons. We would never consider going to a dentist or doctor who said she knew of something potentially more helpful in our current situation but would like to wait until the new year to start prescribing that particular treatment. When one of us (Denise Morgan) was teaching, the book she read for inspiration for implementing a reading workshop was Nancie Atwell's *In the Middle* (1998), in which she shared stories of reading and writing workshops with her middle school students. Denise was teaching second grade at the time but

wanted that same kind of experience for her students. She was constantly changing how independent reading worked in her classroom
as she tried to make sense of it with second graders. She was honest with her students, telling them the reason why she was making
the change. She never really encountered a problem. In fact, on one
Monday a student even joked, "Did you read over the weekend? Are
we changing things again?" We encourage you to get started, to find
time for independent reading regardless of when in the year you are
reading this book.

CHAPTER 3

Managing Independent Reading Programs

Determining a plan to best manage your independent reading program involves thinking through many decisions. For example, how will you choose to record what is occurring in the workshop? Keeping organized is a personal art. It is not uncommon to go through many variations of forms before you find the ones that work well for you. It is a trial-and-error process. Keep your purpose in mind and consider what information you wish to capture, how much space you need to write the kinds of notes you want, and what is the easiest way for you to regularly record and store the information.

RECORD KEEPING

Probably the first step in developing an effective record-keeping system is to develop a list of the kinds of information you anticipate needing. The following sections describe a number of record-keeping tools that might be useful to you during readers' workshop.

Class Conference Summary Sheet

A Class Conference Summary Sheet (Figure 3.1) provides a whole-class overview of whom you have conferred with and the date of that conference. This simple list helps you see when you might have met with a student three times and have yet to confer with another student. The number of spaces across can be tailored to represent

Name	Date	Date	Date	Date	Date	Date

FIGURE 3.1. Class Conference Summary Sheet.

how many conferences you plan to have with each student for each grading period.

Individual Conference Sheet

An Individual Conference Sheet (Figure 3.2) is used to take individual notes on each student during your conference. Each student has his or her own sheet so that it is easy to look across your conference notes for that student over time. It is important to date your conference so you can see over a grading period how often you conferred with a student. By capturing the book title and page number, you have a reference if you even need to revisit that book. You often need the largest space for notes because you will need ample room to record your observations and thoughts. The box at the top right corner can serve as a space for important notes about a child that you might want to investigate or a place to record a pattern you are noticing. The box can also be removed. By regularly taking notes you ensure that you capture important information about the child. You can copy this form back to back to have enough spaces for conferences each grading period.

Future Mini-Lessons

When you confer, you will often come across concepts to revisit. This form (Figure 3.3) lets you list these concepts and decide whether you need to work with an individual or with a small or whole group. When you notice something that needs additional attention or is a new idea, you can jot it down. Then you can decide the best instructional approach for that lesson.

Student Follow-Up Sheet

A Student Follow-Up Sheet (Figure 3.4) helps keep track of students you need to quickly touch base with the day after your conference. For example:

> In your conference with Susi you found out that she was a mere 10 pages from the end of her book. She made a prediction

Name		
Date	Book and page number	Notes

FIGURE 3.2. Individual Conference Sheet.

Teaching possibility	Better as mini-lesson?	Better as small-group instruction?	Possible members for small-group instruction?	Better as whole-group instruction?

FIGURE 3.3. Future Mini-Lessons.

Check in with	About	Notes

FIGURE 3.4. Student Follow-Up Sheet.

Name _____

Date	Title of book	Author
Date	Title of book	Author
Date	Title of book	Genre
Date	Title of book	Genre
Date	Title of book	Genre

Name _____

	Title of book
Monday	
Tuesday	
Wednesday	
Thursday	
Friday	

FIGURE 3.5. Reading Logs for Grades 1–2.

about how it would end and you want to check in with her the next day to see if she was right.

When you talked with Brett yesterday, he was a bit unsure about a possible theme for the book even though he was three-fourths of the way done. You asked him to think about a possible theme and you want to touch base with him quickly the next day to see if has identified one.

In your conference, you asked Julie to find a better book because upon listening to her read and in the follow up discussion, you both came to the conclusion that the book was too hard for her. You asked her to bring a better-suited book to class tomorrow and you want to see what she chose.

Notice that these follow-up conversations are very brief—maybe a minute or two. However, they're important. They enrich your view of your students, and they send children a powerful message: You care about them as readers.

Reading Log

Reading Logs help students keep an account of what they are reading. Figure 3.5 shows several variations of reading logs you may wish to use with your younger readers. Many times it is helpful to create documents that are positioned horizontally so that students have more room to write. You must decide what information you want to capture from each student. Do you want your students to record this information daily? What information do you wish to gather? Do you want students to record the title? The author? The genre? Do you want students to record this information at the end of each period? At the end of the week? If the students are reading chapter books, do you want them to record the page numbers? This is part of the messiness of determining what forms will be right for your students and your goals as their teacher.

Reading logs for older students (Figure 3.6) include much of the same information, but often teachers want their students to record their book information only after they have completed their books. What information do you wish to gather that will be helpful to you as a teacher? That information should be included on the form in _____'s Reading Log

	Date completed	Title	Author	# of pages	Genre	Rating
1.						
2.						
3.						
4.						
5.						
6.						
7.						
8.						
9.						

FIGURE 3.6. Reading Logs for Grades 2–3.

some way. You may ask students to number the books they have read because you want your students to read a certain number of books each grading period. You may want to include page numbers on the form so you can get a sense of the length of the book if you are not familiar with the title. You may want students to record the genre because you expect that students will read from multiple genres. Again, the most important question to ask is, what information do you need from your students about the books they are reading? Your answer will help you modify or create a reading log for your students. You may ask students to rate their book based on a class-designed rating system or a scale of 1 to 10 to see if they are falling in love with their books.

Stop Reading Form

It is natural for readers to begin a book and decide they do not want to finish reading that particular book. Life is too short to read a bad book. A Stop Reading Form (Figure 3.7) can be used as a way to help students think about why they are abandoning a particular book while making plans for the next book to read. This can also help you keep track of how often a child is abandoning a book and what reason the child primarily gives for deciding to abandon the book. As

Name_____Date_____

The book I want to stop reading _____

The reason why I want to stop reading this book _____

The book I am going to begin reading _____

Why I think this book is a better match for me _____

FIGURE 3.7. Stop Reading Form.

with all forms, you can make modifications to better meet your intentions for this information.

Status of the Class Form

You can use a Status of the Class Form (Figure 3.8) daily to quickly record the title of the book and page number for each of your students. Often done after the mini-lesson for grades 3 and up, status of the class (Atwell, 1998) should be a short 2- to 3-minute experience that allows you to learn quickly if a student is making progress in her book. This is also a place to record if a student has forgotten his or her book.

Many times you have to tell the students what to expect when you conduct a status of the class. You might say something like the following:

"Right after our mini-lesson, when I call your name I want you to tell me the title of the book you are reading and the page you are on. I will record that on my chart. We need to do this quickly so make sure you are prepared. I will call your name in

Name	Monday	Tuesday	Wednesday	Thursday	Friday

FIGURE 3.8. Status of the Class Form.

the same order each day so you can anticipate when your name will be called. Ryan, I am always going to begin with you and then Katie, you will be next. Please make sure you are ready to give me that information. This will help me see the progress you are making on the book. If on the next day you are reading the same book, all you need to say is 'same book' and give me the page number. The only time you need to give me the title is when the book is new for you. Any questions?"

We know of teachers who have used stopwatches in the beginning to make doing status of the class game-like so that each day students try and beat their time as a way to help ensure that this check-in does not take too much time.

Status of the class is a quick way to obtain valuable data about your students' reading. For instance, you can see at a glance if a student is having difficulty making progress in her or his book. You will want to check in with a child who is on page 12 on Monday and only on page 18 on Tuesday. You may want to find out why the child has read only 6 pages if students have 30 minutes to read in class and are asked to read for a set amount of minutes at home. Maybe the book is too difficult? Maybe the child is not enjoying the book? By examining your status of the class sheets, you can also look for patterns about children forgetting to bring their books to class. You can know also if a child is a voracious reader. Status of the class is a quick way to check in with all of your students and keep track of what they are reading on a daily basis.

DEVELOPING SUBSTITUTE PLANS

It is never easy to be away from the classroom. Running a readers' workshop can be a challenge for a substitute who is not familiar with the goals and the structure of the workshop. It can be helpful to have a typed explanation about what happens during reading workshop that you can use repeatedly when you are out of the classroom. You could include portions from your parent newsletter that describes what you are doing in reading as a way to further familiarize the substitute with your classroom procedures. Initially, it might take some time to type out your procedures, but once saved on your computer they will require only minor changes as you adjust your workshop. You could explain status of the class and have the substitute record that information. It can be difficult for substitutes to teach a mini-lesson, especially since the lesson is brief. You may choose to forgo the mini-lesson and allow the students to read for the entire workshop time. You will need to prepare the students so they understand that when they have a substitute, they will have more reading time that day. The beauty of the predictable nature of the workshop is that the students understand their role so it can run smoothly if you have to be away.

TROUBLESHOOTING

Regardless of which state or country you live in, similar issues arise for students during independent reading time. Below we share some suggestions for a few of the most common issues we've encountered.

When Students Forget to Bring Their Book Back to School the Next Day

Younger students may have a book bag or folder in which they take books home and bring back the next day. If your students are reading shorter books, it is easy to have a basket of books for children to choose from the following day. Students could also select some books from the classroom library before independent reading begins if they did not bring their book bag back to school.

For older students reading novels this situation becomes more difficult. Since they are reading longer text, it is often not realistic to begin a new book. Having shorter texts available is one solution to this issue. It is nice if students can begin and finish the piece during independent reading time. You could have collections of short stories or books with several short pieces in them like Charlotte Foltz Jones's *Mistakes That Work*, *Accidents Can Happen*, and *Eat Your Words*.

It will help to develop a routine so that students know their options and the expectations if they don't have their book. We all forget things sometimes, so we should not be surprised when a student does also. Sometimes, though, a student frequently forgets her book. You could work with the child to try and establish a system for remembering to put the book into her backpack by determining why the child forgets. Does the child read before bed, putting the book on the nightstand, but forget to transfer it to her backpack the next day? A solution could be to keep the backpack nearby so the child can put the book on the backpack instead of the nightstand before going to bed. By figuring out the child's pattern, you might be able to offer a solution. But sometimes that does not work. You could require that the student find two copies of the same book (by checking another one out from the classroom, school, or public library) and keep one at home and one at school. You could also talk with the child about reading two different books; one book is for home while the other is read at school. Since having a book to read during independent reading is paramount, try to determine what works for an individual child.

When Students Consistently Abandon Their Books

Many times a student will begin a book one day only to inform you he doesn't like his book the next. He chooses another book only to repeat the pattern the following day. It is true that many times readers start and stop books before finding one they really enjoy. Sometimes, though, the child abandons books regularly, never quite finishing a book. You could give a child a reading interest inventory to determine what kinds of books he likes to read. You could personally select several books to book talk to the student, ones you think he will enjoy. You could give the student book reviews to read to find a good match. The student could be encouraged to begin the same book a friend is reading. Sometimes you might simply give the student two books, carefully selected of course, to choose from, limiting the indecision that can arise from too many options. You could also ask the student to check in with you after reading the first chapter (which you have also read) so that you can have an early discussion about the book, establishing a strong understanding about what is happening in the text so far and making predictions about what is to come. Sometimes it takes a little effort to help a student find the right book, but that one right book can be a turning point for a student.

When Students Want to Read Books That Are Too Challenging

Sometimes under the right circumstances a child has enough interest, background knowledge, and motivation to tackle a challenging book. Those experiences stretch him as a reader. While it is good for students to challenge themselves with more difficult books sometimes the book they choose is simply *too* challenging for them. No matter how much the child may want to read a certain book, the book may simply be too difficult. The child reads slowly and makes little progress in the book. Only being able to read a page or two of a 400-page book is simply not enough reading volume. Students need to read a lot each day. One possible solution is to encourage the child to read the more difficult book with a parent at home. Another solution is to help the child understand that while the book is just a little too hard for him now, there will be a time when the book will be a great fit. There is some concern about damaging children's self-esteem if you let them know that they need to find another book. We recognize that this is a delicate balance but, in the end, we are concerned about the child's growth as a reader. We believe that having an honest conversation with the child and helping him select a new book is the best course of action in the long run. Like parents, we have to make difficult decisions that are in the best interest of the child. A child spending weeks or months on a book that is too difficult is, in our opinion, not in the best interest of the child. Just as you would not allow an inexperienced skier to ski the double black diamond course no matter how much he wanted to, we believe helping a child find a more appropriate book is a responsible and necessary action.

When Students Take Too Long to Find Another Book to Read

Most readers know of books they want to read. Often, they have several books to choose from, books given to them by friends, ones they have purchased, and books they want to borrow from the library.

We want students to get into the habit of thinking about their next book so when they finish one, they have several titles to choose from. This is a habit you can encourage students to cultivate. Denise keeps a little notebook in her purse specifically to list books she wants to read next. Whenever she reads a review, hears a friend recommend a title, or sees an interesting book in the bookstore, she records the title. Often students take a long time selecting a new book because they have not done a lot of thinking about their "next book." You could provide students with little notebooks or a sheet that allows them to record possibilities for their next book. You could ask students to spend some time and come up with two or three books they want to read next while noting how they will obtain the books. Students need to know that while they can borrow many books at the library, sometimes books have waiting lists and it might be several weeks before they can check out the book. If you ask students to keep a list of books they want to read, remind them to have their lists handy during book talks so they can easily write down any titles that sound interesting (see Figure 3.9). Talking with students specifically about this helps them understand that having ideas of books to read next is important.

When You Are Behind with Student Conferences

This is a common issue. You set a goal of seeing a certain number of students today and then, suddenly, independent reading time is over

	Title and author	How I will get this book to read
1.		
2.		
3.		
4.		
5.		

FIGURE 3.9. Books I Want to Read.

and you realize that you only met with half of your selected students. The best way to address this issue is to closely examine your patterns while conferring with students.

Do you think your conferences are taking too long? Use a timer to keep track of each conference for several days and look for patterns. What might feel like a 5-minute conference might actual take 10 or 15 minutes. Go a step further by selecting two recent conferences and examine what you tried to accomplish in each one. Were you trying to do too much? Those of you who are feeling brave may wish to audiotape your conferences to see who is doing most of the talking. Are you listening or talking more? You may be trying to squeeze in just one more question or one more comment. Using a timer and/or taping yourself are two ways to examine what and how much is happening during each conference.

Often the most valuable advice or suggestions to issues arising in class will come from the students themselves. By turning over the issue to the individual student or entire class, you can arrive at solutions that feel appropriate to everyone.

When structuring your independent reading program think through the information you wish to collect and the ways you wish to deal with potential issues. By developing and refining your vision for what you want for your students, you will be able to consider what records you wish to collect and how you will address small difficulties as you and your students establish a comfortable routine together.

CHAPTER 4

Ways to Read

This chapter is all about independent reading routines for your classroom. In fact, most of the chapter will offer descriptions of routines that are useful in primary classrooms. But if you are like most teachers we know, you're probably worried about scheduling consistent time for your students to read independently. Time is such a precious commodity in schools; there's never enough. However, we make time for what's important. As you read the bulleted items below, try to develop a rationale for the importance of consistent independent reading in your classroom.

- In 93% of reading comprehension test comparisons, children who read in class or who read more in class performed as well or better than counterparts who didn't read or didn't read as much (Krashen, 2004a). Replacing whatever went on in classrooms with added reading time was just as effective as, or more effective than, traditional instruction in enhancing reading comprehension (Allington, 2000).

- "Collectively, research supports the fact that during primary and elementary grades, even a small amount of independent reading helps increase students' reading comprehension, vocabulary growth, spelling facility, understanding of grammar, and knowledge of the world" (Cullinan, 2000, p. 8).

- A meta-analysis of experimental studies of the relationship between "exposure to reading" (independent reading in any format) and reading achievement provided clear causal evidence that students who have in-school independent reading time in addition to regular reading instruction do significantly better on measures of reading achievement than peers who have not had reading time. Reading time was especially beneficial for students at earlier stages of reading development: students in lower grades, those experiencing difficulties learning to read, and students learning English as a special language (Lewis & Samuels, 2005, p. 2).

• Abundant recreational reading (in and out of school) has been linked to higher achievement test scores, vocabulary growth, and more sophisticated writing styles (see, for example, Block & Mangieri, 2002). Moreover, as few as 15 extra minutes of reading make a difference, especially for struggling readers (Taylor, Frye, & Maruyama, 1990).

We're convinced by the research cited above: Independent reading is well worth the time! Students need daily opportunities to read material of their own choice for their own purposes. Sometimes teachers may want to offer instruction that is related to what children read. Instructional focuses such as learning about concepts about print, learning to attend to rhymes, and so forth, can easily be based on a text that children have read together. Our focus in this chapter, though, is on ways for children to read independently, that is, without your continual direct involvement. We begin by establishing several guidelines for these independent reading routines. We then describe several routines that can be implemented successfully in primary-level classrooms.

GUIDELINES FOR IN-SCHOOL
INDEPENDENT READING

Some choices about how in-school independent reading programs operate may depend on teacher preferences and student need. However, we think the guidelines outlined below apply to all classrooms. For independent reading routines to succeed, students need support, excellent materials to read, an ample and consistent amount of time, and opportunities to share their responses to reading with others.

Students need support to be successful. Elsewhere (in Chapter 2; see pages 37–38) we describe procedures to support children with book selection, such as teaching the "five-finger rule," which helps children learn to select books that are "just right" in terms of their difficulty level. Providing this sort of support may be particularly important for struggling readers (Five & Dionisio, 1999). Avid readers may occasionally be willing to read just about anything, but struggling readers need books they will absolutely love.

It can be tricky to gauge the appropriate level of support for a child, to be supportive without being intrusive. Our goal is successful independent reading, after all, so we don't want to foster unnecessary dependence. Observation and informal conversations can help you learn about the support necessary for children to succeed. Sneak glances at children during independent reading times. Who's consistently day-dreaming or quickly flipping through page after page with seemingly little concentration? Chat with these children. Find out what they like to read and how they select books. By looking and listening, then, you will be able to determine who needs extra support. This may take the form of individual "What did you read today?" chats after the independent reading period concludes, assistance with book selection, access to listening centers, or tutor or buddy reading.

Books and other texts need to be ample, appropriate, and accessible. In Chapter 5 we provide guidelines for establishing a classroom library. In Chapter 3, we describe ways to ensure accessibility, such as putting books in baskets near children's tables. Obviously, easy access to excellent materials to read will enhance any independent reading program. Both the ease of access and the excellence of the texts are important.

Time needs to be considered carefully. To begin with, you will want to decide how much time to devote to what kinds of independent routines. Most of the routines described in this chapter can easily be conducted in 15- or 20-minute sessions.

Next, you will need to think about how to ease students into sustaining the reading for that period of time. In brief, we recommend that you begin with small amounts of time so that everyone can be successful. Then gradually increase independent reading time in 2- or 3-minute intervals until everyone can sustain reading for the amount of time you desire.

Yet the issue is more complicated than simply getting children to 15 or 20 minutes of reading. For example, in response to the question "How much reading do children need?" Dick Allington (2001), former president of the International Reading Association, has said:

> The answer to this question is fluid. This is because the necessary volume of reading seems to shift across developmental stages. In the initial stages, children cannot actually read very much—there is a limited sup-

ply of books they can manage successfully. And young children read much more slowly than older, more experienced readers. (p. 33)

Allington's points, all well taken, should be considered as you determine how much time to devote to independent reading.

The final guideline relates to providing a few minutes after independent reading sessions for children to share with one another. Quick response activities add to the impact of any independent reading routine. Aside from promoting the culture of reading in the classroom, response activities often provide opportunities to prompt recall or help children attend to other comprehension-related issues. Here are several of our favorite response activities (Rasinski & Padak, 2004):

• Hold brief sharing sessions in which a few children read their favorite parts aloud (these are marked with sticky notes as students read). You may want to follow up by asking children why those parts are favorites.

• Ask students to use sticky notes to mark aspects of text for discussion: setting, descriptions, especially powerful language, and so on. Then invite a brief discussion about one of these aspects.

• Ask students to "say one thing" or "say one thing I learned" about their texts.

• Ask students to write interesting words they encounter on sticky notes. Make a class chart or word wall of these. Talk with students about why these are "interesting."

• Play "Around the Room." Announce some aspect of a story (e.g., time, location, main character) and have children tell just this about their books. To reduce time devoted to this activity, you could alternate between boys and girls or between December–June birthdays and July–December birthdays.

• Use large sticky notes inside front covers of books for children to (1) write brief reviews or (2) indicate how much they enjoyed a book using a star system (4 stars…no stars).

• Make a chart for children to write title and number of stars (see above). Ask them to write about the rating in their reading logs.

• Ask children to e-mail their pen pals or parents about the books they're reading.

• Create bookmarks for children to use: "This is the problem in the story" or "This is my favorite part" or "This is my favorite character." Ask them to write on the bookmarks. You might want to provide new book marks, with new ideas for focus, each week or two.

• Select four students' names and direct each one to a corner of the room. The rest of the class goes to a corner as well. The selected student gives a short "commercial" for his or her current book.

• Ask students to write in their reading logs or journals: "What happened in my book today," "what's going to happen next," "my favorite character is," or other general prompts.

Some of these response activities involve whole-group sharing sessions. These can be very time-consuming, so we advise you to approach them carefully. You need to ask yourself whether the time spent is worth it in terms of benefits to students. If a response session exceeds 10 minutes or so, it may need to be revised. One way to shave time from these whole-group sessions is to rotate among the class—ask four or five students to respond each time. Over time, everyone has the opportunity to participate.

INDEPENDENT READING ROUTINES

Readers' workshop and literature circles are instructional routines that support individual students' reading growth and foster the sense of literacy community in a classroom. They are comprehensive routines and thus can form the foundation of your independent reading program. (See Chapters 2 and 3 for more information about readers' workshop.) The other routines described in this chapter—paired reading, buddy reading, reading while listening (or tape-recorded reading), and sustained silent reading—are less comprehensive but also very useful in certain situations. Each routine is described in this section.

Readers' Workshop

Readers' workshops were originally devised for middle school students (Atwell, 1987), but have since been adapted successfully for both older and much younger students (Rasinski & Padak, 2004). Here we focus on what readers' workshops might look like in primary classrooms. Chapters 2 and 3 contain additional information about readers' workshop, some of which is summarized here so that you can compare this routine with the others that are described in this chapter. The two main ideas behind readers' workshops are that (1) students own their reading, including what they'll read and how they'll spend their time and (2) the teacher's role is "as expert reader–writer and guide rather than judge" (Tierney & Readence, 2000, p. 87). The procedure has four elements:

1. Mini-lessons
2. Time to read and write
3. Forums for response
4. Conferences with the teacher

To begin a readers' workshop, you need three things: dedicated blocks of time, ideally daily but at least 2 or 3 times a week; lots of books for children to read; and a plan for helping children participate successfully. You might want to begin with 10- to 15-minute sessions and gradually (within a month or 6 weeks) move to 30- to 45-minute sessions.

The plan for helping children participate successfully might be accomplished through mini-lessons. (See Chapter 2 for additional information.) Mini-lessons to support readers' workshop should be based on what you know children need to know. They can be procedural (e.g., how to select a book that's right for you, things to do during readers' workshop, keeping track of books read) or strategy-based (e.g., what to do if you don't understand). You may also want to introduce response activities during mini-lessons. For example, using a common text you could explore with children how to use sticky notes to "tag" important or interesting information for further discussion. The biggest chunk of readers' workshop belongs to students. They read alone or with partners, share what they have read, respond individually, and so forth. You may want to invite children to practice fluency texts—poems or readers' theater scripts—as well (Padak & Rasinski, 2008). In explaining this period of time to students, you will want to emphasize their freedom to choose. Different students may well be doing different things during a workshop period. Most teachers we know tell children that they are not allowed to do homework or other work during readers' workshop time—they need to be reading or responding to what they've read.

During readers' workshop, you can circulate, observe for assessment purposes, confer with individual students, help individuals select books, pretty much whatever you need to do to foster students' success. As noted in Chapter 3, you may want to create a sheet with students' names and places to record notes. Put this on a clipboard and carry it with you as you circulate while children are in a workshop. This can serve as a place to take notes and also a reminder of who you need to see.

Brief teacher–student conferences are often part of readers' workshop. Individual conferences should be short (no more than 2 or 3 minutes) and focused (see Chapter 2). You will need to decide how often to confer with students. In most cases, once each week is probably enough. The easiest way to control time in a conference is to begin it with a question or request, such as those listed below. Select one (or two) according to what you want to learn about the reader.

- What do you think of this book?
- Who else in our class should read this book? Why?
- Is this book keeping your interest? Why?
- What is this book about?
- (for fiction) Where does it take place? Who are the characters? What is the problem?
- (for nonfiction) What interesting things have you learned? Why are these things interesting to you?
- Read this page out loud to me.

After a conference, make some brief notes about what you noticed—what strengths do you see? What support does the child need? What books/authors might interest the child? Students as well should keep track of how they spend their workshop time. To assist them, you can ask students to keep lists of books read (see Chapter 3). You may also want to establish some expectations for volume of reading, such as requiring that everyone read a certain number of pages per month. You can create a simple form for children to complete and keep in their reading logs: author, title, date read, number of pages.

Literature Circles

Literature circles (Daniels, 2002; Jewel & Pratt, 1999; McMahon & Raphael, 1997; Noe & Johnson, 1999) may be part of readers' workshop or conducted as a separate instructional routine. Literature circles involve small groups of children discussing what they have read. Three models for organizing literature circles work well in primary classrooms. You can use all three at different times for different purposes. The models (based on Fountas & Pinnell, 2001) are:

• *Whole group, same text.* Students read or listen to a common text. Then help students generate topics for discussion. Write the topics on the chalkboard or chart paper and post them where all children will be able to see them. Small, mixed-ability-level groups assemble to discuss these topics. Afterwards, the whole class reassembles to share results of the discussion.

This model works very well as a follow-up to teacher read-aloud. Imagine that you're reading the beginning of *Charlotte's Web*, for example. Possible discussion topics might include (1) should the runt be killed? or (2) what will happen to the runt? (Rasinski & Padak, 2004).

• *Small group, different texts.* In this model, each student reads a different book, but each literature circle's books have something in common. You could form groups according to authors, for example, and have a "Tomie dePaola" group and a "Dav Pilkey" group. Or you could form groups according to content area topics and have an "insect" group and a "mammal" group.

Groups can be formed somewhat randomly; in fact, this model is an excellent way to promote discussions among students of different ability levels. Imagine all the difficulty levels of a set of books about mammals. Children read their individual titles and then meet together with others in their group to share. These discussions ordinarily focus on the common element that provided focus for the group—characteristics of Tomie dePaola's books, for example, or what children learned about insects. As a culminating activity, groups may want to find ways to share what they have learned with their classmates.

• *Small group, same text.* Although you can assign students to these groups in which everyone in each group reads and discusses the same text, giving students some choice might work better. Groups of five or six children work well, so begin by deciding how many titles you will need. (See Chapter 5 for ideas about assembling these text sets.)

Introduce titles by means of brief (no more than a couple of minutes) book talks. Tell children titles and authors. Read an enticing bit of the text or "sell" it in some other way. (More information about book talks is provided in Chapter 2.) List titles on the chalkboard. After you have completed all the book talks, ask each child to make a list of his or her top three choices. Collect these lists and use them to form groups. Not everyone will always be reading his or her first choice, but you will almost always be able to give each child one of his or her top three choices.

GETTING ORGANIZED

After groups are formed, they need to learn how to work successfully. Initial mini-lessons that focus on how successful groups operate can be helpful, as can occasional discussions about what children have learned about good discussions. Some teachers we know post class-generated "rules" for good discussions on posters.

As children are becoming accustomed to working in small groups, you may want to suggest ways to proceed. For example, you may want to suggest that children try reading their texts aloud in their groups before discussing them and also try reading texts beforehand (e.g., during sustained silent reading or readers' workshop). Then they can decide which model they prefer.

With longer texts, you or groups can decide how much of the text to read at (or before) a literature circle discussion. If children make their own decisions, they will want to check occasionally to decide if they're reading too much or too little between sessions. Sticky notes or reading journals can be helpful tools for children to keep track of issues they want to discuss.

THE ROLE OF ROLES

Some teachers find that helping children assume roles in discussions can facilitate their learning how to conduct discussions independently.

That is, roles may serve as a scaffold, a temporary assist, as children learn about how literature circles work. Possible roles include:

- Group leader—leads discussion, encourages everyone to participate, keeps track of time.
- Summarizer—begins discussion by briefly summarizing the text or portion of the text.
- Comparer/Connector—compares text to other texts or to real life.
- Sentence or Word Finder—finds and shares interesting sentences or words.
- Questioner—develops and shares questions about the text.
- Predictor—leads discussion about upcoming portions of the text (Rasinski & Padak, 2004).

You may find that it's best to introduce these roles gradually and to create situations for alternating who performs what role so that children can learn about all of them. Careful observation will help you decide when to encourage children to move from formal roles to more open-ended discussions. Eventually, the roles often begin to stifle natural conversation instead of facilitating it. This is the time to offer children options about whether or not to continue with formal roles.

EVALUATION

Observation is a wonderful tool for evaluating children's performance in literature circles. Decide beforehand about what to observe—text-related comments, ways children build on others' comments, evidence of having comprehended, enthusiasm/ engagement, and so on. If your school district or state has standards to guide instruction in literacy and language arts, look at your standards for speaking and listening for you will find literature circles a great context for learning about these aspects of your students' language use.

An easy way to keep track of your observations is to make a blank chart with what you will be observing down the side and spaces for children's names across the top. Each time new literature circles are formed, make and complete a chart for each group. Brief notes or evaluative symbols (O = outstanding; S = satisfactory; U = unsatisfactory) should suffice.

Sometimes, all groups have problems. Suppose you were in a book club with a few friends and a few strangers. Now suppose that one book club member consistently tried to lead the conversation away from the topic at hand. Another seemed disengaged all the time. Still others talked either too much or too little. One person was even rude or dismissive if she disagreed with another's comments. What would you do? Initially, you would probably be patient with these problems. You would realize that becoming a functional group takes some time. But what if the negative behaviors persisted? Might you decide to leave the group?

Children don't have the option to leave their literature circles. Besides that, one goal for literature circles can be to help children learn to communicate effectively. So you'll need to develop some strategies for helping children learn to work productively. Although we have no sure-fire solutions for the problem of dysfunctional groups, we do have a few ideas:

• Be patient. Watch carefully for a while to see if the group can "right" itself. If this happens, be sure to tell children what you observed and to praise them for their success at self-regulating.

• Spend more time than usual sitting close to the dysfunctional group. Don't join the group because this will most likely hamper conversation; children will start looking to you to provide feedback or answers. Sit near the group, however, as this sends a subtle signal to children, who will sense your presence and may begin to work more productively.

• Talk privately with group members. In a nonjudgmental way, tell children what you have observed. Say, for example, "I've been noticing that two people in this group seem to do all the talking, and two others hardly ever make any comments. What do you think about this? Does this seem like a problem to you? If so, how can I help you find solutions?"

• Hold occasional mini-lessons about positive group dynamics. Help children learn how to express disagreement agreeably. Ask them to brainstorm solutions to problems they have had. Post solutions on your Rules for Good Discussions chart.

As we mentioned earlier, readers' workshop and literature circles can form the foundation of your independent reading program. The routines we describe next—paired reading, buddy reading, listening while reading, and sustained silent reading—may not be as foundational, but they are still useful. Each description addresses the purpose of the activity, advice about materials, steps in the basic procedures for the activity, and options and hints about adaptations that you may find useful.

Paired Reading

Purpose: to provide individual reading support

Materials: anything the student wants to read

Procedures:

1. Student selects book.
2. Student and a good reader (classmate, older student, volunteer, parent, etc.) read the book aloud and together.
3. Student and good reader decide on a signal (e.g., tap) to indicate that student wishes to read alone. If student wishes to read alone, good reader follows silently. If student makes a mistake, good reader joins in again.
4. Good reader's voice slightly leads if student needs a great deal of support. Good reader's voice slightly follows if student needs little support.
5. Student logs paired-reading activities (length of time, pages read, assessment of ability, etc.)

Options and Hints:

- Paired reading works well with classroom volunteers or in peer tutoring situations.
- Encourage children to evaluate partners and themselves by asking them to respond to such questions as: Was the reading smooth? Did the reader use his or her voice to show meaning? Did the reader know the words? You could use smiley and frowny faces to create an easy response slip. (See Figure 4.1.)
- If you are going to pair children, try creating a list from the most able reader to the least able reader. Then divide the list in half,

Name_____ Date _____

Was my reading smooth?

Did I use my voice to show meaning?

Did I know the words?

What did my partner think of my reading?

FIGURE 4.1. Sample Evaluation Sheet. Next to each question, draw three simple faces: smiley, straight-lined mouth, frowny.

pair the top of each half, and so forth. Of course, you could also invite children to select their own partners, perhaps allowing them to work together as long as they can do so productively. In any event, the less able reader in each pair should select the text that the pair will work with.

- You will need to think about how to handle absences and decide what you'll do if pairs have difficulty getting along (Vacca et al., 2005).

Buddy Reading

Purpose: to provide an authentic reason to practice reading; to develop readers' self-esteem; to provide listeners with good models of oral reading.

Materials: texts selected by the younger of the buddy pairs (see below).

Procedures:

1. Pair up students from two grades. Before buddy reading officially begins, you may want to provide pairs with opportunities to get to know each other and each others' interests.
2. Teacher of younger class helps children select books for their buddies to read.
3. Teacher of older class provides these books and time for older buddies to practice reading them. Discussions about how to hold

books so that younger children can see the illustrations and how to talk productively about the content of the books may be useful.

4. Once each week or two, the buddy pairs get together for reading sessions. After each session, the routine begins anew.

Options and Hints:

- A parent volunteer (or two) can easily organize this program.
- Buddies may want to become pen pals.
- If interest warrants, older students can make word games or puzzles to play with their younger buddies.
- Evaluation should focus on both sets of students.

Reading While Listening (Tape-Recorded Reading)

Purpose: to provide individual and independent practice in fluency

Materials: books with accompanying audiotapes. The tapes can be commercially produced, such as those that can be checked out from a library. Another alternative is to develop a classroom listening library by having students prepare tape-recorded versions of classroom books for their peers to read.

Procedures:

1. Create a listening center in the classroom. Headphones and tape recorders will work best.
2. Stock the listening center with engaging texts/tapes for students to read while they listen.
3. Provide students with 15 to 20 minutes per day at the listening center.
4. Help students select books that (a) are written at their instructional levels and (b) are very likely to be engaging.
5. Remind students to follow along in the text as they listen.
6. Students may want to log the pages they read during each session.

Options and Hints:

- Older students or volunteers can make additional tapes to be added to the listening center.
- Invite students to select books to read on tape. Ask the student reader to practice enough times until his or her oral reading of the

book is fluent. (It's easy to tape over a version that either the student or you want to change.)

- Invite students to read aloud (whisper-read) along with the voice on the tape on occasion.
- You can evaluate the impact of this activity by observing student involvement. To gauge growth, you could also ask students to read a page or two from a book, both before and after they have worked with it in the listening center.

Sustained Silent Reading

Sustained silent reading (SSR), along with its aliases (DEAR [Drop Everything and Read] and SQUIRT [Super Quiet Independent Reading Time], among others), has been a staple in many classrooms and schools since the 1970s. It is, simply, a time when everyone reads—children and adults alike. SSR can be schoolwide or within only one classroom. If SSR is schoolwide, it's usually at the same time each day. Start and stop times are often indicated by a signal of some sort over the public address system.

Purpose: to promote sustained involvement and engagement in reading. SSR is particularly useful in situations in which some children do not select reading as a free-time activity. Being together with a group of people who are reading provides strong motivation to read.

Materials: anything to read of the child's choice. These can be books, magazines, electronic resources—any reading material. Decide whether you will permit children to reread something they've previously read, such as a favorite book or a text that you have used instructionally. (We recommend that you allow repeated readings, but it's up to you.) Young children will need several books for each SSR session. You may want to provide library time before SSR begins, or you may want to scatter baskets of enticing books around the room within easy reach of a child who may need a new book.

Procedures:

1. You might want to have SSR at the same time each day until children become accustomed to it.
2. Begin by talking with children about SSR—what it is and why it's important. Also explain the rules: everyone reads during the entire

SSR time; children need to select books beforehand because they can't spend SSR time looking for books.

3. Make sure that you read while the children are reading. During other independent reading routines we describe in this chapter, you may be doing other things. During SSR, though, read! And here's why:

> Several studies have shown that, if SSR classes are observed in the middle of the school year, about 90% of the students are reading and that the probability that students will actually read is increased when several factors are present—among them access to interesting reading material and teachers who read while children are reading. (Krashen, 2005, pp. 446–447)

4. Use a timer to begin and end each session. When the timer goes off, you may want to say, "Let's take another minute. Get to a good stopping point."

Options and Hints:

- Beginning readers or children who need extra support during SSR can do whisper reading or buddy reading.
- You may want to combine SSR and letting children read for the same amount of time during the day but at times they choose. For example, you may want to have SSR three times each week and let children select when to read for 15 to 20 minutes on the other 2 days. To decide this issue, watch children for a while. If everyone can read independently and successfully, then you may not need as much everyone-at-once SSR. If not, then perhaps SSR makes sense (Cunningham & Allington, 1999). Of course children's ability to sustain their reading may change over the school year, so you will want to check again every month or so.
- You may want to ask children to keep simple logs of the books they read during SSR: title, author, number of pages, date. Then you can use these titles occasionally during reading conferences with children to assess their ability to remember what they've read, reread fluently, identify unknown words, and so on.
- Many teachers find that SSR works well as a bridge to other independent reading routines, such as readers' workshop. If you and your students are unaccustomed to "just reading," SSR is a great

way to begin because the structure helps children get into the reading habit. Eventually, though, you may want to shift toward readers' workshop.

SOME FINAL THOUGHTS

We began this chapter talking about time. We end that way, too. As you plan how to incorporate these independent reading routines into your instruction, decide on a schedule that will work for your students and you. Some teachers alternate readers' workshop and literature circles each week using a M-W-F versus T-Th schedule. Others may ask students to work in literature circles at the beginning of each week and in readers' workshop at the end (M-T-W versus Th-F). Still others rotate these routines every 2 or 3 weeks—all literature circles until everyone is finished, then all readers' workshop for a similar length of time, then back to literature circles, and so on. Each of these works well, so think about which makes most sense to you.

Having decided on the major routines, you will then want to think about other possibilities. Which of your students could benefit from paired reading or reading while listening, for example? When can these activities be scheduled? If you use learning centers, either of these could be good activities. Buddy reading may take the place of literature circles or readers' workshop one day each week. Perhaps you can find 10 or 15 minutes each day for SSR as well.

All together, then, you may want to devote about an hour each day to independent reading routines. As we pointed out at the beginning of the chapter, this will be time well spent. Research is clearly pointing to the achievement-related benefits that are related to volume of reading. That's not the whole story, though. Independent reading routines foster "literacy-rich" classrooms, a place where all children deserve to learn:

> Children who are successful at becoming literate view reading and writing as authentic activities from which they get information and pleasure.... They know what reading and writing are really for and they want to be successful at it. The literacy-rich classroom communicates the importance of real reading and writing activities by engaging children in a variety of print activities and not relegating reading and writing to a brief period. (Cunningham & Allington, 1999, p. 21)

CHAPTER 5

Creating Classroom Libraries

What do you like to read? How were your reading preferences shaped? How do you obtain your reading material? You probably steer clear of reading material that is too difficult unless you have a serious need to read it, right? We are all avid readers, yet our reading preferences differ.

Thinking about our own choices and behaviors as avid adult readers can offer insights into our work with children. Perhaps you were lucky enough to encounter teachers along the way who nurtured your motivation to read. That's the point of this entire book: Teachers can and should help students become avid independent readers. This chapter focuses on "what" to read—issues related to selecting books for children and providing an inviting classroom library.

Research has offered some insight into the importance of selection and access—the two major topics of this chapter. For example, library centers with lots of inviting books, coupled with teachers' planned activities with books, lead to:

- Preschool and kindergartners' interest in books (Morrow, Tracey, Woo, & Pressley, 1999; Pressley, Rankin, & Yokoi, 1996; Taylor, Pearson, Clark, & Walpole, 1999).
- Vocabulary gains for low-socioeconomic-status students at grades 2, 4, and 6 (Snow, Barnes, Chandler, Goodman, & Hemphill, 1991).

Some teachers beat the odds; each year their students perform far above expectations. Naturally, researchers are interested in these teachers and their classrooms, instruction, and so forth. Finding out what happens in these classrooms can provide research-based advice for others; some results of these studies of exemplary teachers underscore the importance of selection and access as well. These teachers have clearly defined, well-stocked book areas and lots of child-produced print. Children have lots of time/ encouragement to interact with books (Loughlin & Ivener, 1987; Pressley et al., 1996).

Your classroom library can become a sort of magnet to draw children into books. In this chapter we use the development of a high-quality classroom library as a focus for considering issues related to book selection and access. The chapter is organized around five questions, the satisfactory answers to which should help you steer your students to the road to independent reading.

HOW MANY BOOKS SHOULD WE HAVE IN OUR CLASSROOM LIBRARY?

One way to assess a classroom library is "by the numbers." Here are three answers to this question about quantity, all from reputable sources:

• "School library media centers should have at least 20 books per child and classroom libraries at least 7 books per child" (International Reading Association, 1999).

• "If I were required to establish guidelines for quantity, I would recommend at least 500 different books in every classroom with those split about evenly between narratives and informational books and about equally between books that are on or near grade-level difficulty and books that are below grade level." (Allington, 2000, p. 55)

• In their research on the TEX-IN3 instrument, designed to determine the effectiveness of classroom literacy environments, Hoffman, Sailors, Duffy, and Beretvas (2004) found three levels of quantity; inadequate (1–7 books per child); basic (8–19 books per child); and outstanding (20 or more books per child). Hoffman et al. note, as well, that higher ratings are associated with higher standardized test scores.

Hoffman et al. and Allington recommend about 20 books per child. We think this is an admirable goal.

WHAT KINDS OF BOOKS SHOULD WE HAVE IN OUR CLASSROOM LIBRARY?

In addressing this question, most experts argue for large and balanced collections, for, as Fountas and Pinnell (2006) note "A strong collection of books is the foundation for effective instruction that helps students become competent readers" (p. 194). This makes sense. Would you be eager to read materials that were of no interest or that were too challenging?

Balance is a good goal for collecting books likely to be of interest to children. Vacca et al. (2005) suggest five different types of titles:

- Modern and realistic fiction.
- Classic fiction.
- Books that feature diversity (e.g., different ethnic and cultural groups, nontraditional families). To select multicultural literature, teachers are advised to examine accuracy, authenticity, purposeful inclusion of characters and situations, and nonstereotypical treatment of characters.
- Collections that will work with instructional themes.
- A variety of nonfiction, both for general interest and for topics to be studied in content areas.

To this list, we add:

- Poetry books.
- Predictable literature.
- Series books.

Moreover, classroom libraries should contain books for instruction as well as books that children can read independently (Cullinan, 2000). In their study of effective literacy environments, Hoffman et al. (2004) found three aspects of variety related to achievement test gains, as seen in Table 5.1.

The classroom library should contain ample titles for students of differing reading abilities and interests (Cullinan, 2000), so the difficulty level of books in your classroom library deserves attention. Materials should support and encourage young readers; for primary-

TABLE 5.1. Variety of Texts in Classroom Libraries

Aspect	Inadequate	Basic	Outstanding
Nonnarrative books	10% or less	10–20%	20% or more
Publication dates	Less than 30% in last 3 years	30–50% in last 3 years	50% or more in last 3 years
Availability of multiple copies	None	Few	Many

level children, lots of predictable texts and other easy-reading books should be a goal (Rasinski & Padak, 2004). Gambrell, Wilson, and Gantt (1981) found that error rates at or higher than 5% (see Figure 2.6, p. 37) were associated with off-task behavior. As Krashen (2005) notes:

> The way all of us developed our reading ability was through extensive reading of texts that did not require strain and suffering and that were so interesting that we were completely absorbed in the message. Delayed gratification is not necessary to learn to read and to improve in reading. (p. 447)

All of this advice suggests that classroom libraries should be full of easy, interesting books.

HOW CAN I FIND GOOD BOOKS TO ADD TO THE CLASSROOM LIBRARY?

Having thought about how many and what kinds of books should be in your classroom library, the next step is deciding on particular titles. This can be a daunting task; thousands of new books for children are published each year. Fortunately, several handy resources exist for finding good books. A primary resource is other professionals: the school and public librarians and veteran teachers. Librarians are accustomed to locating great books for children; in our experience, they are delighted to share what they have learned about wonderful new titles. Veteran teachers also typically know which titles are engaging.

Professional journals are another good source for teachers in search of good books. *The Reading Teacher (RT)* and *Reading Today*, both published by the International Reading Association (*www.reading.org*), have articles or columns about new children's literature, as does *Language Arts*, published by the National Council of Teachers of English (*www.ncte.org*). In addition to regular columns, *RT* also publishes "Children's Choices" each October; this is a report of recently published books that children from across the United States have rated as their favorites.

The figures that follow provide ways to begin looking for titles for the classroom library. Figure 5.1 lists websites devoted to children's

www.ala.org/ala/alsc/awardsscholarships/childrensnotable/notablecbooklist/ currentnotable
  Notable children's books, shared by the American Library Association

www.monroe.lib.in.us/childrens/booklists
  Booklists by grade levels

www.reading.org/resources/tools/choices
  Children's Choices winners

www.nea.org/readacross/resources/catalist
  Teachers' top 100 books, compiled by the National Education Association

www.carolhurst.com/titles/allreviewed
  Carol Hurst's children's literature site

www.hbook.com/resources/books
  The *Horn Book*'s list of recommended children's literature

www.cbcbooks.org/readinglists/childrenschoices/booklists
  Children's Book Council booklists

www.ucalgary.cas/~dkbrown/awards
  Calls itself "the most comprehensive guide to English-language children's book awards on the Internet"

www.bookspot.com/readinglists/childrens
  A site that lists dozens of other sites

www.planetesme.com
  A site from author Esme Raji Codell

FIGURE 5.1. Some great websites for learning about children's literature.

literature (all active as of July 2007). You may want to bookmark these lists on your computer so that you can return to them often.

Figures 5.2–5.5 are a series of starter lists for types of books frequently found in primary-level classroom libraries: concept books, predictable or patterned literature, series books, and poetry.

One final and excellent source for titles of books to add to the classroom library is your students. Ask children to share particularly interesting titles. If they receive books as gifts or use the public library, ask them to be on the lookout for "brilliant, breathtaking books," those that absolutely must be added to your classroom collection. To keep track of books to acquire, you may want to keep a card file or a list on your computer.

HOW CAN I AFFORD TO PURCHASE THESE BOOKS?

This is a tough question to answer satisfactorily. We don't know a single teacher who feels that he or she has enough money to purchase all desired books. Still, some creative searching often brings success. Here are some ideas for acquiring books:

- Share with colleagues. Perhaps you and another teacher at your grade level can swap titles midyear, thus providing children in each classroom a new set of books to explore.
- Request funds to purchase books from your school's parent organization.
- Go early to "friends of the library" sales. Identify yourself as a teacher.
- Sponsor a read-a-thon where children get pledges for number of pages read. Use the proceeds to buy books.
- Ask for parent donations of books their children have outgrown.
- Go to yard sales, garage sales, and thrift stores. Leave your phone number with employees at thrift stores; ask someone to call you when children's books arrive.
- Ask students and parents to donate books in lieu of birthday treats.
- Use bonus points from book clubs (Scholastic, Troll).

Alphabet Books

Bridwell, N. (1984). *Clifford's ABC*. New York: Scholastic.

Ehlert, L. (1993). *Eating the alphabet*. New York: Harcourt.

Feelings, M. (1974). *Jambo means hello*. New York: Dial.

Geisert, A. (1986). *Pigs from A to Z*. Boston: Houghton Mifflin.

Grimes, N. (1995). *C is for City*. New York: Lothrop, Lee and Shepard.

Hoban, T. (1987). *26 letters and 99 cents*. New York: Greenwillow.

Johnson, S. (1995). *Alphabet city*. New York: Viking.

Kitchen, B. (1984). *Animal alphabet*. New York: Dial.

Laidlaw, K. (1996). *The amazing I spy ABC*. New York: Dial.

Marshall, J. (1995). *Look once look twice*. New York: Ticknor and Fields.

Martin, B., & Archambault, J. (2006). *Chicka chicka boom boom*. New York: Simon & Schuster.

Musgrove, M. (1976). *Ashanti to Zulu*. New York: Dial.

Pelletier, D. (1996). *Graphic alphabet*. New York: Orchard.

Tapahonso, L., & Schick, E. (1995). *Navajo ABC*. Boston: Little Brown.

Winter, J. (2006). *Calavera Abecedario: A day of the dead alphabet book*. New York: Voyager.

Colors

Boynton, S. (1984). *Blue hat, green hat*. New York: Simon & Schuster.

Ehlert, L. (1988). *Planting a rainbow*. New York: Harcourt.

Hill, R. (1986). *Spot looks at colors*. New York: Putnam.

Hoban, T. (1988). *Of colors and things*. New York: Greenwillow.

Jonas, A. (1989). *Color dance*. New York: Greenwillow.

Lionni, L. (1959). *Little blue, little yellow*. New York: Astor.

McMillan, B. (1988). *Growing colors*. New York: HarperCollins.

Reasoner, C. (1996). *Color crunch*. New York: Putnam.

Walsh, E. (1989). *Mouse paint*. New York: Harcourt.

Counting

Addshead, P. (1996). *One odd old owl*. New York: Child's Play.

Boon, E. (1996). *1, 2, 3: How many animals can you see?* New York: Orchard.

Bowen, B. (1995). *Gathering: A northwoods counting book*. Boston: Little Brown.

Falwell, C. (1993). *Feast for ten*. New York: Clarion.

Giganti, P. (1992). *Each orange had eight slices: A counting book*. New York: Greenwillow.

Hoban, T. (1985). *1, 2, 3*. New York: Greenwillow.

Kitchen, B. (1987). *Animal numbers*. New York: Dial.

Long, L. (1996). *Domino addition*. Watertown, MA: Charlesbridge.

Merriam, E. (1996). *12 ways to get to 11*. New York: Alladin.

Pallotta, J. (1992). *The icky bug counting book*. Watertown, MA: Charlesbridge.

Ryan, P. (1994). *One hundred is a family*. New York: Hyperion.

Tafuri, N. (1986). *Who's counting*. New York: Greenwillow.

Wadsworth, O. (1985). *Over in the meadow*. New York: Viking.

FIGURE 5.2. A starter list of concept books.

Adams, P. (2000). *This old man*. New York: Child's Play.

Ahlberg, J., & Ahlberg, A. (2003). *Each peach, pear, plum*. New York: Viking.

Brown, M. (1947). *Good night moon*. New York: Harper & Row.

Brown, M. (1949). *The important book*. New York: Harper & Row.

Brown, R. (1981). *A dark, dark tale*. New York: Dial.

Carle, E. (1994). *The very hungry caterpillar*. New York: Philomel.

Carle, E. (1977). *The grouchy ladybug*. New York: Crowell.

Cowley, J. (1999). *Mrs. Wishy-Washy*. New York: Philomel.

Williams, S., & Vivas, J. (1996). *I went walking*. New York: Harcourt.

Gag, W. (1928). *Millions of cats*. New York: Coward-McCann.

Galdone, P. (1973). *The little red hen*. New York: Scholastic.

Hennessy, B. (1990). *Jake baked the cake*. New York: Viking.

Hill, E. (1980). *Where's Spot?* New York: Putnam.

Hutchins, P. (1968). *Rosie's walk*. New York: Macmillan.

Hutchins, P. (1986). *The doorbell rang*. New York: Greenwillow.

Keats, E. (1999). *Over in the meadow*. New York: Penguin.

Kraus, R. (1970). *Whose mouse are you?* New York: Macmillan.

Martin, B. (2007). *Brown bear, brown bear*. New York: Holt.

Numeroff, L. (1985). *If you give a mouse a cookie*. New York: HarperCollins.

Peek, M. (1985). *Mary wore her red dress & Henry wore his green sneakers*. New York: Houghton Mifflin.

Raffi. (1988). *Down by the bay*. New York: Knopf.

Sendak, M. (1962). *Chicken soup with rice*. New York: HarperCollins.

Seuss, Dr. (1957). *The cat in the hat*. New York: Random House.

Shaw, N. (1988). *Sheep in a jeep*. Boston: Houghton Mifflin.

Wescott, N. (1980). *I know an old lady who swallowed a fly*. Boston: Little Brown.

Williams, S. (1992). *I went walking*. New York: HarperCollins.

Winter, J. (2000). *The house that Jack built*. New York: Dial.

Wood, A. (1996). *The napping house*. New York: Scholastic.

Zemach, M. (1972). *The teeny tiny woman*. New York: Scholastic.

FIGURE 5.3. A starter list of predictable literature.

WHAT SHOULD OUR CLASSROOM LIBRARY LOOK LIKE?

In a series of studies involving hundreds of children, Morrow and Weinstein (1986) found that very few preschool and primary-age children independently chose to read. This means that we need to support children's reading habits—make it as enticing for children as possible and help children be successful.

Access to books appears to be an important feature of this support. In fact, Palmer, Codling, and Gambrell (1994), who used questionnaires and interviews to find out about what motivates children

Adler, D. *Cam Jansen* books. New York: Penguin.
Allard, H. *Miss Nelson* books. Boston: Houghton Mifflin.
Asch, F. *Bear* books. New York: Scholastic.
Bridwell, N. *Clifford* books. New York: Scholastic.
Brown, M. *Arthur* books. Boston: Little, Brown.
Clifton, L. *Everett Anderson* books. New York: Holt.
Giff, P. R. *The Kids of the Polk Street School* books. New York: Random House.
Hill, E. *Spot* books. New York: Putnam.
Lobel, A. *Frog and Toad* books. New York: HarperCollins.
Park, B. *Junie B. Jones* books. New York: Random House.
Parrish, P. *Amelia Bedelia* books. New York: HarperCollins.
Rey, H. A. *Curious George* books. Boston: Houghton Mifflin.
Rylant, C. *Henry and Mudge* books. New York: Simon & Schuster.
Rylant, C. *Mr. Putter and Tabby* books. New York: Harcourt and Brace.
Sharmat, M. *Nate the Great* books. New York: Random House.
Zion, G. *Harry* (the dirty dog) books. New York: HarperCollins.

FIGURE 5.4. A starter list of series books.

to read, found access to be one of four powerful influences on motivation. Children wanted easy access to books; they said having books available in the classroom library was particularly important.

The first step in providing access is to have a classroom library. Find a spot in your classroom that you can devote to housing children's books. Lowe (2005) recommends that this decision be based on student traffic patterns: "If students can easily move in and out of the library, or if they need to pass through it, they'll often get sucked in by an exciting cover." Other ideas for organizing the classroom library follow:

- Use stickers or labels for difficulty level, genre, and so on.
- Use tubs to store books by theme, genre, and author.
- Display front covers. Rotate these "featured" books often. Attend to the visual appearance of the library.
- Put series books, genre, or multiple copies for buddy reading or literature circles together.
- Start a books-on-tape collection.
- Make name magnets for young children. Keep a metal filing cabinet near the library, so children can use their name magnets to check out books by affixing book cards to metal with magnets.

Carle, E. (1989). *Eric Carle's animals, animals*. New York: Philomel.
dePaola, T. (1988). *Tomie dePaola's Mother Goose*. New York: Putnam.
deRegniers, B., Moore, E., & White, M. (1988). *Sing a song of popcorn*. New York: Scholastic.
Dyer, J. (1996). *Animal crackers: A delectable collection of pictures, poems, and lullabies for the very young*. Boston: Little, Brown.
Hale, G. (1997). *Read-aloud poems for young people*. New York: Black Dog and Leventhal.
Lansky, B. (1994). *A bad case of the giggles*. New York: Meadowbrook.
Lansky, B. (1996). *Poetry party*. New York: Meadowbrook.
Lobel, A. (1986). *The Random House book of Mother Goose*. New York: Random House.
Moss, J. (1989). *The butterfly jar*. New York: Bantam.
Moss, J. (1991). *The other side of the door: Poems*. New York: Bantam.
Prelutsky, J. (Ed.). (2000). *The Random House book of poetry for children*. New York: Random House.
Prelutsky, J. (Ed.). (1999). *The twentieth century children's poetry treasury*. New York: Random House.
Silverstein, S. (1974). *Where the sidewalk ends*. New York: HarperCollins.
Silverstein, S. (1981). *A light in the attic*. New York: HarperCollins.
Slier, D. (Ed.). (1996). *Make a joyful noise: Poems for children by African American poets*. New York: Scholastic.
Sword, E. (2006). *A child's anthology of poetry*. Hopewell, NJ: Ecco.
Viorst, J. (1981). *If I were in charge of the world and other worries*. New York: Atheneum.

FIGURE 5.5. A starter list of poetry books.

Ideally, children should handle all aspects of the library's operation. This process can begin with a mini-lesson or two about how the classroom library is organized. Ask children to help you devise a check-out system. Rotate who is in charge of monitoring it, as well as who will reshelf returned books. By taking responsibility for their classroom library, children will develop feelings of ownership about its contents—the books!

The goal is for the classroom library to be visible and accessible. It should be set apart somehow from the rest of the classroom. It should be full of titles that beg to be read. As you think through plans for developing your classroom library, particularly related to book selection and access, we recommend that you keep this advice, from Fountas and Pinnell (2001) in mind: "A richly varied classroom collection will enable your students not only to expand their reading abilities but also to expand their world" (p. 89).

CHAPTER 6

Independent Reading
and Students with Special Issues

Independent reading is often thought of as an activity that is most applicable for students who are average or above-average achievers in reading. These students need the freedom and opportunity to explore literature on their own without the hindrances of assignments, worksheets, or class discussions. Readers who struggle are often viewed as incapable of engaging in independent reading. They are seen as needing the teacher's close monitoring or direct involvement while they read, respond, and engage in other reading-related activities. Allington (1977, 1978, 1983a, 2000) argues compellingly that struggling readers are often the ones who get the fewest opportunities to engage in authentic reading; as a result, he asked the pointed question, "If they don't read much, how they ever gonna get good?" (Allington, 1977, p. 57)

Although struggling readers may need additional and more focused reading instruction, we believe that students who struggle in reading need independent, authentic reading as much as their more advanced reading peers. Indeed, these students may be in even more need of authentic, independent reading. When reading instruction is too often controlled by the teacher and when it involves primarily activities that are not real reading, such as word list reading, worksheets, and the like, students may develop a sense that reading is nothing more than a set of isolated skills that need to be practiced repeatedly, or something that provides little satisfaction. Indeed, the lack of authentic reading and the overemphasis of nonreading reading activities may lead students to avoid reading altogether. Poor performing readers tend to be more disenchanted with reading than higher achieving readers, and this may lead them to avoid authentic reading. Lack of authentic reading may create a vicious cycle that leads to even less reading over time.

In this chapter, we explore the role of independent authentic reading with students who may not be the best readers in the class. We make the case that authentic independent reading, if done with care and consideration, can have a dramatic impact on students who struggle—both in terms of their reading and academic achievement and in terms of their personal attitudes toward reading.

WHAT MATTERS IN LEANING TO READ

The publication of the report of the National Reading Panel (2000) galvanized interest in reading around the country. For the first time, a national body of experts told educators and the American public what really matters when it comes to teaching reading. The panel identified five components that are keys to success in learning to reading—phonemic awareness, phonics or word decoding, vocabulary or word meaning, reading fluency, and comprehension. Although we know that there are other factors associated with success in reading, the National Reading Panel's list is a good starting point.

If success in learning to read requires instruction in each of these areas, then it may be inferred that students who experience difficulty in learning to read may exhibit difficulties in one or more of these areas, which will require additional instruction and support. Independent reading can be tailored to provide additional support to students in each of these areas. In subsequent pages, we explore how this can be done.

An Irony

Before we move into an exploration of making the National Reading Panel's recommendations work in independent reading, we need to address one other conclusion of the Panel. In its report, the Panel indicated that there was no evidence that independent reading was associated with student success in reading. Implied in this conclusion was that independent reading should not be part of a school reading program: Teachers can do independent reading with their students, but it should not be considered part of their core reading curriculum.

Obviously, such a conclusion flies in the face of the direction of this book. We think that independent reading is essential to success in reading. Common sense tells us that the act of reading is bound to improve one's ability to read. Moreover, in previous chapters we have provided ample evidence that supports the efficacy of independent reading for students.

We feel that the Panel did not fully explore the data, or at least make an informed attempt to explain their lack of significant findings. We think that the Panel's findings can be easily explained: The research the Panel chose to examine included only studies that featured experimental and control groups. In other words, the many studies showing a relationship between reading volume and reading achievement (e.g., Postlethwaite & Ross, 1992) were not included in the Panel's analysis. Moreover, independent reading was sometimes not associated with significant gains in reading achievement because students were likely not reading independently—they were more likely faking it.

Most informed teachers are aware that during independent reading time, some students may be putting on a good show. They may be sitting quietly with a book in front of their faces, but not really reading. They may be daydreaming, doodling, or doing something other than reading itself. So, if they weren't reading, one should not expect to find any gains in reading achievement.

The key to success in independent reading is to make students accountable for this precious time. In the previous chapters, we have described ways in which this can happen—by the teacher conferencing with students about what they read, by students being asked to provide an oral summary to the group, by students keeping a daily response log, and so on. The act of reading does improve one's reading—teachers just need to make sure that students actually read. In addition, as we show below, independent reading can contribute to children's development in other essential areas of reading.

PHONEMIC AWARENESS

Phonemic awareness refers to the ability of readers to essentially conceptualize language sounds—that is to be able to not only hear but also think about the sounds of language, to blend sounds into words, to segment sounds from words, to identify sounds and their locations within words, and so forth (Mraz, Padak, & Rasinski, 2007). Phonemic awareness is an early reading competency that is essential to further growth in reading. For students to profit maximally from phonics instruction, phonemic awareness is a necessity. If students are unable to blend individual language sounds into words, or to manipulate the sounds of language in other ways, phonics will become an enormously difficult competency to master.

Independent reading (read by children themselves or with a parent) provides wonderful opportunities to help children develop this competency. The key is in the type of text chosen. Nursery rhymes and other rhyming poems as well as tongue twisters or alliterative texts are natural sound plays. Read repeatedly, as children are apt to do, young readers will certainly begin to notice various features of language. Consider the following:

> Betty Botter bought some butter,
> "But," she said, "the butter's bitter.
> If I put it in my batter,
> It will make my batter bitter.
> But a bit of better butter,
> That would make my batter better."
> So she bought a bit of butter,
> Better than her bitter butter,
> And she put it in her batter,
> And the batter was not bitter;
> So 'twas better Betty Botter
> Bought a bit of better butter.

If a student were to read or listen to this poem several times, he or she would definitely begin to notice the sound of *b* that is repeatedly articulated in the poem. Indeed, a brief conversation would be all that is needed to help youngsters notice the sound, how it is articulated in the mouth, and perhaps even the written letter that represents the sound.

> Little boy blue come blow your horn,
> The sheep's in the meadow the cow's in the corn.
> But where's the boy who looks after the sheep?
> He's under a haystack fast asleep.
> Will you wake him? No, not I—for if I do, he's sure to cry.

"Little Boy Blue" offers children the opportunity to explore several sound features in a rhyme that is certain to be read repeatedly. Certainly, the rhythmical nature or the full text becomes apparent through multiple readings. Beyond that, however, children may begin to notice the same *b* alliteration found in "Betty Botter," the *r*-controlled vowel *or*, the long *e* and long *i* vowel sounds, and of course the *eep* word family.

Later when, just for the fun of it, children begin to read or have read to them "Little Bo Peep," they will begin to notice similar language sound features that are also present in "Little Boy Blue." They may also notice other similarities between the texts—letter sound relationships and even words. Children who have repeated opportunities to explore these texts with parents or others are certain to have a head start on phonemic awareness and early reading over children not given such opportunities.

Many students who struggle in reading, younger and older, English speakers and English language learners, do not have sufficient phonemic awareness to profit maximally from phonics. As a result these students do not become efficient word decoders, and this in turn negatively impacts the development of fluency, vocabulary, comprehension, and overall reading achievement. Opportunities for young readers to listen to, read, reread, and explore rhymes and other texts that play with the sounds of language is one of the best ways to develop phonemic awareness and to ensure that all students get off to a good start in reading. For struggling readers, reading texts of this sort will help them overcome any concern in phonemic awareness that may be contributing to other problems in reading.

PHONICS

Learning to sound out or decode words is one of the primary tasks of learning to read. One cannot read unless he or she can turn the printed words into their oral representations. Many children (and older students) struggle with this competency.

Research is telling us that one of the best ways to decode words is by identifying common combinations of letters that consistently represent a language sound or sounds (Adams, 1990; Cunningham, 2004; Ehri, 2005; Gaskins, Ehri, Cress, O'Hara, & Donnelly, 1996–1997; Gunning, 1995; Snow, Burns, & Griffin, 1998). The most common, and perhaps useful, of these letter combinations are what teachers call word families or phonograms. Psychologists have termed them *rimes*. We will use the more common term *word family* in this book. A word family is simply the part of a syllable that begins with the sounded vowel and contains any subsequent letters within the syllable. Thus, in the word *cat* the -at is the word family and in the two-syllable word *batter* the two word families are -at and -er. There are several advantages in using word families to teach phonics. First, they are remarkably consistent: -at says at in nearly all one-syllable words in which it appears and in most multisyllabic words as well. Second, word families are efficient. Readers who employ word family strategies process words in multiletter chunks as opposed to the letter-by-letter processing that is used in other forms of word analysis and decoding. Third, word families worth learning are found in a remarkably large number of English words.

There are literally hundreds of word families worth teaching, and students who can recognize these word families in single and multisyllabic words have the ability to process such words accurately and efficiently. Edward Fry (1998) demonstrated the utility of word families in his list of the "most common phonograms."

-ab	-at	-ill	-op	-unk
-ack	-ay	-im	-ore	-y
-ag	-ed	-in	-ot	
-ail	-eed	-ine	-out	
-ain	-ell	-ing	-ow (how, chow)	
-am	-est	-ink	-ow (bow, throw)	
-an	-ew	-ip	-uck	
-ank	-ick	-ob	-ug	
-ap	-ight	-ock	-um	

According to Fry, knowledge of the word families listed above gives a reader the ability to decode and spell 654 one-syllable words simply by adding a consonant, consonant blend, or consonant digraph to the beginning of the word family. Beyond one-syllable words, knowledge of these word families can help readers at least partially decode thousands of words in which these word families regularly appear. For example, the rime *-am* can help a reader with words like *ham*, *Sam*, *slam*, and *jam*. The same word family can also help a reader with more challenging words such as *Abraham*, *Amsterdam*, *bedlam*, *camera*, *hamster*, *grammar*, *telegram*, and many more. The value of word families in helping students decode words is enormous.

As with phonemic awareness, there are texts that lend themselves naturally to independent reading and provide remarkable opportunities for students to explore word families. Because words families tend to rhyme, brief rhymes or poems are the texts of choice for learning word families. Moreover, the brevity and rhythmical nature of most poetry make these passages fun to read over and over and easy to master, even for the most struggling reader. Consider the following poem by Robert Louis Stevenson:

"At the Seaside"

When I was down beside the sea
A wooden spade they gave to me
To dig the sandy shore.
My holes were empty like a cup,
In every hole the sea came up,
Till it could come no more.

This poem would provide students with opportunities to explore the *-ore* and *-up* word families. Other poems and rhymes feature other word families for students to read and explore. Following up students' reading of rhymes with discussions about the word families they may have encountered will help solidify their awareness and understanding of word families.

A poetry corner in every primary grade classroom is an ideal place for children to discover and play with word families. Here, young poets can find and read poetry that the teacher has collected. In addition to book collections of poetry, individual poems can be organized in a file drawer by word families so that children can choose poems that match a particular word family that is being studied in class.

Moreover, since simple rhymes generally follow a rhythmical pattern, students can easily write their own poems. These student-composed poems can be rehearsed and eventually performed for the class.

Independent reading, in all its forms and with all kinds of reading material, can lead to improved word decoding. As students read they may come across words they can't pronounce. These are the words that can prompt focused instruction on how unfamiliar words can be solved. Students should be instructed to keep a journal or reserve a section of their literature response journal to record words with uncertain pronunciations or meanings—words to be solved. Periodically, the teacher (or parent or aide) will meet with individual or small groups of children to work through the words they have chosen. The teacher can show children how these unknown or interesting words can be decoded or what they mean. The teacher may also provide other information such as the history of the words or other meanings or uses of the words. When the words chosen for instruction are words that the students themselves choose, the students are much more likely to become engaged in learning how to solve the word and how that knowledge can be applied to other words that share similar characteristics.

Word decoding or lack of adequate phonics skills is the key concern for many struggling readers. Independent reading of natural decodable texts, authentic texts that have embedded in them the phonics elements that struggling readers must master, provides teachers and parents with another way to help the struggling reader make up for lost ground, feel successful, and find enjoyment once again in reading.

VOCABULARY

Vocabulary is the flip side of phonics. It is not enough for students to be able to decode or sound out a word; they also need to know the meanings of the words they read. Otherwise, those words that they decode are nothing more than nonsense words.

A vast array of words exist in the English language. This means that authors have a multitude of words to choose from when they write. Therefore readers of English need to have knowledge of a variety of word meanings. Understanding words is a complex task in the English language.

For some struggling readers, vocabulary is a significant issue. Students with limited life experiences and exposure to language and the world are likely to have limited meaning vocabularies. This then results in poor or limited comprehension of texts that students read. This is particularly true for English language learners, who may have excellent word decoding skills from their native language that can be applied to English. However, their knowledge of the meanings of the English words is likely to be lacking.

Strong vocabulary programs and instruction in elementary and middle schools are clearly called for. However, vocabulary instruction can effectively be supplemented through independent reading. Cunningham and Stanovich (1998) point out that the literature that children and adults read is filled with wonderful words that have the potential to build vocabulary. In written texts, vocabulary is generally more sophisticated than the vocabulary found in oral speech. Authors, on purpose, include more interesting and less common words in their written texts in order to improve their writing and clarify their message. This may be why the National Reading Panel (2000a) concluded that indirect vocabulary learning is such a powerful way to increase vocabulary.

Thus, the materials that children and adults read provide a rich base for vocabulary learning. Moreover, the rich contexts in which the words are found (accompanying words, phrases, sentences, paragraphs, illustrations, etc.) aid readers' comprehension. The very act of students reading on their own; reading with a partner; or listening to a text read to them by a parent, teacher, or through a prerecording provides opportunities to increase vocabulary.

Most authors embed a rich array of words in their writing. One of our favorite authors is William Steig. Just in the first few pages of his book *Caleb and Kate*, a picture book intended for primary grade children, readers will find words such as *cantankerous*, *departed*, *odious*, *swollen*, *pondering*, *breeches*, *traipsed*, *cronies*, and many more. Although these may be challenging words, their meanings can be accessed through the general context of the story. Few children fail to understand the story, and even fewer fail to add to their vocabularies or deepen their knowledge of words already in their vocabularies by reading this book or having the book read to them.

Although the act of reading such material will increase students' knowledge of words, this learning can easily be enhanced by asking students to become aware of the words they think are interesting. Blachowicz and Fisher (2005) describe vocabulary-rich classrooms in which teachers ask students to find words that are interesting while reading independently or being read to by the teacher. These words are "harvested" regularly and written on a sheet of chart paper. The teacher and students talk about the chosen words, elaborate on their meanings, and use them in sentences. Throughout the day, reference is made to the words, and students are asked to use the words in their own speech and writing.

We think an excellent and simple way to capitalize on daily independent reading is to reserve 5 minutes after the designated reading period for students to share, on a large sheet of chart paper, the interesting words that they have found. These can then be explored in a number of ways—used in oral and written language, practiced throughout the day, sorted in various ways (by grammatical category, by number of syllables, by meaning, etc.), used in various classroom games such as word bingo or twenty questions, and sent home for additional practice.

Imagine, if students (and the teacher) chose 10 words every day from the texts they were reading independently, over the course of a 180-day school year, students would be exposed to nearly 2,000 interesting words—words they have chosen from the texts they have been reading by choice. Not only would vocabulary be certain to expand, students would most certainly develop a greater appreciation for well chosen words that good authors are always on the search for. And this focus on words embedded in rich, authentic, engaging, and meaningful contexts is exactly what will help struggling readers and children learning English as another language.

FLUENCY

Reading fluency takes the notion of word expertise to a higher level. With phonics and vocabulary instruction the aim is to develop a high level of accuracy in students' knowledge of an ever expanding body of words. However, it is not enough for students to simply develop accuracy; they need to develop fluency with words and text.

Fluency refers to the ability to read words effortlessly or auto-matically (Allington, 1983b; Rasinski & Hoffman, 2003). All read-ers have a limited amount of cognitive energy that they can give to the task of reading. Reading also requires the simultaneously opera-tion of at least two cognitive tasks—recognizing the words in the text and comprehending the author's overall message. Cognitive resources given over to one task in reading cannot be applied to another. Stated more practically, if a reader has to employ too much of his or her cognitive energy to the word recognition task in reading, she or he may not have sufficient cognitive resources left to make sense of the overall passage. Comprehension fails not because the reader does not have the cognitive ability to make sense of the text, but because the reader has used too much cognitive ability in the lower-level task of word recognition.

There is another aspect of fluency that is often neglected in instructional programs for teaching fluency. Linguists call it *prosody*. Teachers call it *reading with expression*. Readers make meaning by using their voices during oral reading—to phrase text appropriately (to mark sentence and phrase boundaries) and to employ intonation, volume, rate or speed, pausing, and emphasis to add to the written message.

Both aspects of reading fluency are strongly associated with growth and achievement in reading (Rasinski, 2004; Rasinski & Hoffman, 2003). Moreover, research has shown that the lack of read-ing fluency is one of the chief concerns among students who struggle in reading. Rasinski and Padak (1998) found that a measure of read-ing fluency was the most distinguishing characteristic of elementary students referred for Title I reading intervention because of perceived difficulties in reading by their teachers. Duke, Pressley, and Hilden (2004) suggest that readers' difficulties in word recognition and flu-ency are major contributing factors in the lack of reading achieve-ment for a large majority of readers who struggle.

Research has pointed out the repeated reading and assisted read-ing are the most promising instructional methods for teaching read-ing fluency (National Reading Panel, 2000a). In repeated readings, students read a selected passage repeatedly until they achieve a level of proficiency. Once achieved, they move on to another passage to practice repeatedly. Assisted reading involves reading a passage while simultaneously hearing a fluent rendering of the same passage read by another. Activities involving reading fluency also improve students' word decoding as well as comprehension.

While fluency lends itself well to direct instruction, independent reading, in its various forms, can also be employed to help students overcome difficulties in fluency.

Perhaps one of the best and simplest ways to help students develop an internal awareness of the full nature of fluency is to hear fluent reading. Of course, this is best accomplished by the teacher (or other proficient reader) reading to students in as fluent a voice as possible. All students love to hear a teacher or parent read to them. Part of the enjoyment comes from hearing the fluent reader make the passage come alive with his or her voice.

To make the read-aloud experience even more focused on fluency, the teacher may often follow up the read-aloud with a discussion of how meaning was made by raising or lowering his or her voice, making a dramatic pause, increasing or decreasing reading rate, or emphasizing a particular word or phrase. The teacher may discuss with students how those actions added to the meaning of the text by asking, for example, "What were you expecting to happen next when you heard me pause for several seconds at this point in the story?" or "What did I do at this paragraph to help build the excitement and tension that the author wanted to convey in the story?" This kind of talk will help students see that reading fluency means making meaning, not just reading the words accurately or quickly. And if students see that fluency is an integral part of the passages that are read to them, they will see that they too need to strive to read with a similar degree of fluency to make meaning.

The aim of fluency is to read text with automaticity and prosody. One way to achieve both is through practice or rehearsal, or what S. Jay Samuels (1979) termed repeated reading. Ideally, as students read a text repeatedly, they develop automaticity over the words and phrases they are reading; they also develop prosody as they learn through repeated readings of a text to use their voices to make meaning.

Perhaps the most authentic situation for engaging in repeated reading or rehearsal is performance. Actors, singers, poets, musicians, and other performers willingly engage in rehearsal in order for their ultimate performances to be as good as possible. Thus, we view oral performance of a text as an authentic and natural reason for engaging students in repeated readings. Moreover, a large part of the practice or rehearsal can and should be done independently, with students practicing on their own or in small groups without the specific direction of the teacher.

Naturally, a key to performance reading is using texts that are meant to be performed. Poetry, rhymes, songs, speeches, scripts (readers' theater), jokes, dialogues, and monologues are particularly well suited for oral presentation to an audience. Other texts that are written in a strong voice such as narratives, letters, journals, and diaries are also well suited for performance, as readers must strive to make the author's voice come alive in the performance.

Imagine a classroom where every Friday afternoon the class engages in a weekly readers' theater festival, poetry café, songfest, or the like. The routine begins every Monday, however, when students, individually or in small groups select (or write) a script, poem, song, speech, letter, or other passage that they will rehearse all week and perform on Friday. The teacher provides time throughout the day for students to engage in rehearsal, on their own or in small groups. The aim of the rehearsal is not to read the passage accurately or quickly (this will come with practice); rather the aim of the rehearsal is to read with appropriate expression or prosody so that the listening audience will appreciate the students' performance. Although students work independently during these rehearsal periods, the teacher is constantly monitoring the students—helping with selection of texts, modeling fluent reading, providing feedback, making suggestions, and giving encouragement.

On Fridays, the last hour of the school day is reserved for the performance. The classroom is transformed into a theater or coffee house, replete with refreshments provided by volunteer parents. The school principal is invited as well as other classrooms and parents. Students help with transforming the classroom for the performance, setting the agenda, and other planning. The weekly performances become the highlight of the week for both students and teacher. They become a fond school memory that will remain with the children for the rest of their lives.

Assisted reading also can play a role in the performance routine that we have just described (Rasinski & Hoffman, 2003). As mentioned earlier, assisted reading involves a student reading a text while simultaneously hearing it read fluently. The other reader could be a teacher, teacher aide, parent, older student, or classmate. Children could also read chorally with a group or even listen to a prerecorded version of the text on a tape recorder or other recording device. Assisted reading could even involve something as unusual as watching television with the closed captions displayed on the television screen.

The possibilities for employing assisted reading with independent reading are many. Situations can be created where students spend dedicated time in assisted reading of material of their own choice with the express purpose of reading for enjoyment. Students could read with an assigned partner, or read while listening to prerecorded material for as little as 10 to 15 minutes daily.

In the performance routine that we described earlier, assisted reading could be used in the rehearsal phase. After students have been introduced to a text that will be performed, and before they have achieved sufficient fluency on the text to practice it on their own, they can practice the passage in an assisted reading format—focusing on smooth and expressive reading. Students could practice the text while listening to it read by the teacher or other more fluent readers. Eventually, students could read the passage without assistance.

Fluency in reading has been the neglected goal of the reading program—for years it was not a priority in reading curricula. Research over the past several decades has reversed this perspective. Fluency is clearly an important part of learning to read, and many struggling readers have difficulty achieving fluency. Readers who do not achieve fluency will most likely struggle with, dislike, and avoid reading their entire lives. Integrating a focus on reading fluency into independent reading will certainly make a difference in the reading lives of many students who struggle to achieve high levels of literacy.

COMPREHENSION

Comprehension is, without question, the goal of reading and reading instruction. We want students to be able to make meaning from what they read. Students who have difficulty in the areas of reading that we have described earlier in this chapter will likely also experience difficulty in comprehending what they read. Phonemic awareness contributes to students' ability to decode words, and, in turn, word decoding, vocabulary, and fluency all contribute to comprehension. So, nurturing growth in these areas will lead to improved comprehension. But attention to those areas is not enough.

Some students who appear proficient in word decoding, vocabulary, and comprehension may still have difficulty in comprehension. For these struggling readers, comprehension itself may be the concern. They may not have sufficient background knowledge to handle the content of the passage, or they may not know or employ comprehension strategies that would help them to attain meaning from what they read.

For these students, a focus specifically on text comprehension is called for. Teachers will work directly with students to build their background knowledge and to teach them specific strategies for making meaning from text. However, in addition to direct instruction, we feel that independent reading can go a long way toward improving students' ability to make meaning from what they read. Indeed, research has demonstrated that students who are given regular opportunities to read independently do make significantly greater gains in comprehension and vocabulary than students who spend their time in other reading-related activities such as worksheets and drill (Cohen, 1968).

Building Background Knowledge for Comprehension

There are two major pillars in reading comprehension—background knowledge and comprehension strategies (Rasinski & Padak, 2007). Background knowledge simply means that a reader needs to know something about what it is he or she is reading. Most of us have had the experience of reading something on a topic that is relatively foreign to us. Even though we may be able to read the words accurately and fluently, even though we know what the individual words mean, we experience difficulty in understanding what we have read. The reason is that we have little pre-existing knowledge of the content of the passage to connect with or relate to the new content.

Some students, because of a variety of circumstances, may not have sufficient background for much of their reading. Perhaps they come from impoverished circumstances where they have limited opportunities to experience the world. Or, perhaps they come from another land or culture and have not yet become familiar with the world and culture that is represented in the text. For these and other students for whom background knowledge is an issue, increasing background knowledge is a priority.

Fortunately, one of the best ways to build background knowledge is to read and be read to. Teachers and parents can and should use read-aloud time to build students' background knowledge. We recommend choosing material that children will not only find interesting but that will also help them expand their knowledge—both world knowledge and literary knowledge. The ever-growing body of literature for children and adolescents, especially in the area of informational texts, means that there are very few topics for which a teacher cannot find high quality read-aloud material.

Picture books are particularly valuable for building background knowledge. By nature, picture books are relatively short and can be read in a few minutes. Moreover, more and more picture books on informational topics are being produced. This means that teachers have a wide and growing body of these brief and engaging texts that are certain to build interest and background for nearly any topic and content area—from math to science to history.

Read-alouds should also be a time for teachers to explore genre that students might not normally be drawn to in their own reading. Some students may choose to read realistic fiction or informational or expository texts on their own. During read-aloud time, then, teachers can introduce students to fantasy, science fiction, historical fiction, biography, poetry, and the many other types of literature that they may not have much experience with. Because teachers do the reading to students and provide cognitive support for the passage, they can often stretch and challenge students with materials that may be somewhat above their students' reading levels.

After reading a book or section of book to students, teachers can simply lead a brief discussion that will help solidify students' understanding of the text. Conversations that focus on such tasks as summarizing the text, critiquing the passage, comparing and contrasting it with other passages, and of course using the information from the passage in some way will not only strengthen students' background on the topic, but will initiate the use of comprehension strategies for making meaning from the text.

Students can also read independently to build background knowledge. Teachers can help this process by making books and other reading materials available for students who are focused on a particular topic that requires background building. The teacher may bundle several books, magazines, and other reading texts together, place them on a shelf in the reading corner of the classroom, and require that during independent reading time students select one or more items from the bundled material to read. Later, students can work in a group to share the information they have obtained from their own reading with others in the group so that a number of students can gain from the reading of multiple texts. All of us build our background knowledge by reading and being read to by others. For students whose background knowledge is not adequate and who, as a result, struggle in learning to read, building background knowledge through the teacher reading to students and students reading is essential.

Building Comprehension Strategies

Once students have background knowledge in place, they need to use it to make meaning from the texts they read. The process of making or constructing meaning usually involves the use of a process or strategy. Among important strategies are predicting, comparing and contrasting, question asking and answering, summarizing, responding creatively to reading, monitoring comprehension, and cooperative learning and reading. All of these strategies are usually part of a direct instruction program in comprehension. In the next several paragraphs, we provide examples of how these important strategies can be easily woven as well into various forms of independent reading.

PREDICTING

When a reader makes a prediction, he or she is essentially inferring information that is not explicitly stated in the passage; the reader is using background knowledge as well as the text to make meaning. Inferential comprehension is often thought of as a higher form of comprehension than literal-level comprehension. During teacher or parent read-aloud, prediction can be encouraged by the teacher or parent simply coming to a natural stopping point in the text and asking, "What do you think will happen next in this story? Why do you think so?" To answer such questions, the reader has to engage in some sophisticated thinking, orchestrating both the text and his or her background knowledge.

Similarly, prediction can be encouraged during student independent reading by asking the same two questions. Students could be asked to end every independent reading session by writing in their reading journal their response to those two important questions. Conferencing with students after independent reading, either individually or in groups, provides excellent opportunities for teachers to ask students to make predictions about upcoming events in the stories they are reading.

Comparing and Contrasting

When readers compare and contrast what they are reading with another text or compare some element from what they are reading with something from another book, in their own lives, or in the world they live in, they are engaging their minds in sophisticated analysis of the text that leads to deeper understanding of what they have read. In reading we have come to call such comparisons text-to-text, text-to-self, and text-to-world connections. For read-aloud or independent reading, students can be prompted before the period to be sure to make a connection between their reading and something outside of the text itself. The deep analysis and meaning making comes when students explain their connections, whether through talk or in writing. "Why is this text like another book I have read? How is this character like me? How is this episode in my story like and unlike an event that occurred in my school several days ago?"

Asking and Answering Questions

Question asking and answering have been found to be powerful tools to nurture comprehension. Traditionally, we have often thought of students answering questions posed by the teacher to be the essence of comprehension instruction. However, more recent thinking suggests that the creation of thoughtful questions can be just as important, if not more important, than the actual response to the question itself.

As with prediction and compare and contrast, questioning is a central part of instructional programs for reading comprehension and can easily be integrated into classroom read-aloud and students' independent reading experiences. Simply prompting students to create questions as they read and writing them in their literature journal is all that is required. Teachers can specify the types of questions—focused on plot, character, scene, mood, writing style, and so on. Moreover, the levels of questions that students create should be more at the inferential and critical level, not literal. "I wonder" is often a good prompt to get students thinking well beyond the facts of the story, to use their background knowledge along with the information from the text to make thoughtful and meaningful responses. Indeed, to get students thinking at the higher levels, we recommend that teachers frequently model from their own reading the kinds of high-level questions that they want students to create.

Once students have created questions, they can also be prompted to answer or respond to the questions they or their classmates have created. The process of developing, then responding to high-level questions requires the kinds of sophisticated thinking that lead to deep understanding of what has been read.

SUMMARIZING

Summarizing what has been read clearly requires text understanding. But, to summarize well, a student needs to sort through all the information in a passage, identify the important ideas, and then organize those ideas into a coherent reflection of the overall text. Summarizing can be quite challenging for many students, but the more opportunities students have to summarize will yield better summaries and deeper comprehension. Thus, independent reading provides more chances for students and teachers to explore how texts can be summarized succinctly and well.

In independent reading, students should be asked to periodically summarize what they have read, in writing or speech. Summaries can be a daily occurrence, taking place at the end of the read-aloud or independent reading periods. Teachers can alter the ways that the summaries are made—limit the summary to one, two, or three sentences, no more than 50 words, use only 10 important words to identify the main points of the passage, or create a diagram that summarizes the passage.

Picture books often provide wonderful examples of summaries for students. Indeed, pairing up a longer text that students read independently with a picture book of the same story that the teacher may read to the class is a great way to demonstrate how the author of the picture book has summarized the longer story that the students are reading. The picture book can be analyzed and compared with the more elaborate text to understand how the picture book author was able to retell the same story, but in many fewer words than the other author.

Another fine example of a summary is found in nearly every book published in the United States. It is the Library of Congress summary that you will find in the front matter of most books. In a few sentences, the writer of the summary is able to distill the nature of the book. Children will find it interesting (and helpful) to see that the very books they read for independent reading themselves contain summaries of the content of the book.

RESPONDING CREATIVELY

Response to reading can take a variety of forms—from activities such as retelling or writing a summary, discussing the story with classmates, writing in a journal, doing some worksheets, taking a quiz over the content of the story to simply thinking about the passage over a period of time. Creative response to a text, however, means being a bit more open in how a student may react to a passage that has been read. In responding to a text a reader creates something new that is in some way related to what has just been read. This can be in the form of creating a piece of artwork in response to the story, rewriting the story as a script to be performed as a reader's theater, developing a game based on the story, or retelling the story as a newspaper article, a letter to the editor, an advice column, or a television advertisement. Recreating the text in another form, whether visual or performing art or other form, requires students to think deeply about the meaning expressed by the author and how they can express the same meaning in another form.

Creative response to reading is a natural for independent reading, which does not usually have preassigned response activities associated with it, so asking students to respond to what they have read in some creative form can both engage and liberate them. Students who may not respond well in traditional ways are allowed to use their creative energies to demonstrate their own understanding and to make their own form of meaning from a passage they have read.

MONITORING COMPREHENSION

Good comprehension means monitoring one's own meaning making. Good readers are aware when their understanding of a passage is not where it should be and, once they become aware, they take steps to remedy their lack of comprehension. To complicate matters, acceptable comprehension depends somewhat on purpose for reading. Imagine reading directions for installing something, say a Global Positioning System (GPS) for your car. You might read the directions once quickly to see if you could install it yourself; then, when you are actually doing the installation, you might read the same directions quite differently. So what "counts" as acceptable comprehension differs in the two situations, even with one reader and one text.

Since comprehension and comprehension monitoring take place inside a reader's head, these are often difficult to teach directly. Nevertheless, read-aloud and independent reading provide excellent opportunities to explore comprehension monitoring with students. During the regular classroom read-aloud periods, the teacher can, through think-aloud episodes, demonstrate for students his or her own process of monitoring reading comprehension. If comprehension falters, the teacher can stop and explain this to students. He or she can then explain the steps that will reestablish understanding. The teacher can also demonstrate, through this think-aloud process, other metacognitive activities that occur "in the head" while reading—making connections to other texts, self, and the world, making predictions, and so on.

Independent reading is also a good time to nurture comprehension monitoring. After an independent reading period, students can be asked to write about or share with classmates their own comprehension monitoring processes that occurred while they read. What were they thinking about? What problems did they encounter? How did they overcome those problems? Making these metacognitive processes visible for all students will help them monitor their comprehension, thus improving their comprehension overall.

COOPERATIVE LEARNING AND READING

Finally, comprehension can be fostered through cooperative learning and cooperative reading activities. When students teach one another, when they help one another with academic tasks, the student receiving the help clearly benefits, but the student providing the assistance and instruction is also benefiting. To explain something to a classmate, a student needs to work through his or her own understanding of the task or content. The process of working through task or content is the act of comprehending.

Throughout this section of the chapter we have been sharing comprehension strategies and how they can be nurtured through independent reading in all its forms. One form of independent reading is partner or group reading—when students pair up or group together to read a text. This can take the form of simply sitting with a friend during sustained silent reading, alternating pages that are read aloud. Or, it can be as elaborate as a group of students working through and rehearsing a script together in preparation for the readers' theater festival at the end of the week. No matter how it happens, cooperative reading and learning makes students responsible for one another's understanding of the passage read. And this responsibility leads all students to think deeply about what they read and to share their understandings, predictions, comparisons, questions, summaries, responses, and comprehension problems with others. All of the strategies we have described earlier in this section can be integrated very effectively into cooperative learning and reading activities.

Before we leave comprehension, let us share one last thought. The strategies we have described are important for all readers. However, for students who struggle in comprehension, learning and using these strategies are critical. Employing these strategies during independent reading makes excellent sense so we should remind students to use them. Fortunately, the strategies may even be embedded in the texts that students read.

Earlier in this chapter, we mentioned that picture books often provide excellent examples of summaries of longer texts. Similarly, reading material can be found that nurtures predictions; that provides examples of compare and contrast; or that contains examples of good questioning, creative response, summaries, and cooperative learning. Other texts lend themselves well to student questioning, reader creative response, student summaries of longer pieces of information, and cooperative learning and reading activities. By grouping texts together along these lines and asking students to use them in their independent reading, we will provide additional support, especially for students who need help in becoming better comprehenders of what they read.

A CLOSING THOUGHT

One of the main goals of independent reading is to develop in students a genuine love for reading. As students read materials for their own purposes and at their own times, they will begin to see that reading has intrinsic value, and they will want to continue reading throughout their lives. However, independent reading can also be molded and shaped to assist our instructional efforts in reading, especially those efforts aimed at helping struggling readers. In this chapter, we have explored how the five essential components of effective reading instruction can be strategically extended through independent reading. We hope you will choose to use independent reading to not only expand students' love for reading but also to help all students become the proficient readers they deserve to be.

CHAPTER 7

Assessment and Monitoring Issues in Independent Reading

In our previous chapter we discussed how independent reading can be used to reinforce skills that have not sufficiently developed in some students who struggle in learning to read. Difficulties in these areas are the cause of their struggles in reading. Reading and reading-related activities aimed at these areas of concern during independent reading can help students make significant progress in these reading competencies and lead to accelerated general growth in reading. Assumed in the previous chapter was of teachers the ability to identify areas of concern and be able to measure growth in reading over time.

Assessment is the topic of this chapter. We will consider how teachers can use authentic reading activities, similar to the kind of reading experienced during independent reading, to identify areas of strength and weakness in reading, measure growth in reading achievement over time, and identify students' current reading levels in order to match students to materials that they can read successfully. In addition to these assessment issues, we will explore how teachers can monitor students' independent reading over time. It is important for teachers to know the amount of independent reading students do so that they know to intervene with those students who may not be reading as much as necessary. We will begin this chapter, however, by focusing on students' reading interests. We explore how teachers can identify students' reading preferences so as to match them with materials that match their interest, not just their reading level.

ASSESSING READING INTERESTS

Independent reading works best when readers have the opportunity to read material that taps into their personal interests. Even as adults, we tend to gravitate toward those materials that reflect our interests. Some readers enjoy contemporary fiction, others historical fiction, still others gravitate toward nonfiction, biography, poetry, personal advice, inspirational, and all the other genres available. Some readers find greatest satisfaction in books, while others prefer magazines, newspapers, and still others like to do their reading on their computer screens.

For your independent reading activities to be successful, you need to match students' materials to their interests. Of course, this means that you need to know students' interests. Learning students' interests in reading is an assessment issue. Once interests are learned, you can stock the classroom shelves with those materials; you can also ask the school librarian to ensure that such materials are readily available in the school library; and, of course, you can provide parents with this information so that they can make sure that such interesting material is available at home.

We think that the best way to tap into students' interests is to simply ask them what turns them on about reading—what are their likes and dislikes when it comes to reading and what are the conditions under which they most prefer to read. Asking students questions about interests and preferences can be done orally in a one-on-one conference, or it can be done with a large group of students who respond in writing to the questions posed. The key to gaining access to students' interests is having the right questions to ask. In the Reading Interest Inventory in Figure 7.1 we have assembled 10 interest-related questions that, through our own experience, provide excellent opportunities to learn about students' interests in reading.

Some students will provide elaborated responses to these questions; others will be more reticent. For those who are less responsive, you may want to follow up with more questions. However, you need to understand that some students may not be aware of their interests or the conditions that are most favorable for their own reading—they haven't thought much about those things in the past. The simple act of asking these questions, perhaps at the beginning of the year, and

Directions: Present the following questions to students, either in a personal interview or as a written survey for all the students in your classroom. Analyze the results to determine your students' main interests in reading.

1. Do you like to read? Please describe as best you can why you like or do not like reading. What could I (the teacher) do to make reading more enjoyable for you?

2. Do you like reading more or less than a year ago? What caused you to change how you feel about reading?

3. What are the names or titles of your favorite books, books that you either read or that have been read to you by your parent or teacher?

4. Do you have a favorite author? What is his or her name?

5. How do you find books and other materials that you choose to read?

6. Do you like prefer stories or books that are more informational?
   a. What types of information topics interest you the most?

7. Out of the following types or kinds of books, which is your favorite? Which is your second favorite? Which do you like the least?
   a. Fairytales and folktales.
   b. Stories about children your own age (contemporary fiction).
   c. Biographies (true stories about famous people).
   d. Fantasy and science fiction.
   e. Informational books (books that give you information about things and tell you how to do and make things).
   f. Joke and riddle books.
   g. Historical fiction (stories about events in history).
   h. Poetry.

8. Do you like to read magazines?
   a. Name the magazines that you like the best.
   b. What topics do you like to read about in magazines?

9. In your own words, please describe the kinds of reading materials you like the most.

10. In your own words, describe the conditions under which you most like to read—do you like it quiet or noisy? Do you like to hear music in the background while you read? Do you like bright lights or not so bright? Do you like to read alone or with others around you? Do you like to read at your desk, or do you prefer a comfy chair or a pillow on the carpet?

11. Do you ever read a book, story, or other reading passage more than once? If so, why do read something more than one time?

FIGURE 7.1. Reading Interest Inventory.

---

then again at the midpoint of the year, and once again at the end of year, provides students with opportunities to think about their own interests in reading, to think metacognitively about how they perceive reading, and to notice changes in their reading preferences over time. This awareness of their own reading interests helps nurture a mature awareness and attitude about reading that will guide students in their reading and reading choices throughout their lives. And, by administering the interest inventory at several points throughout the year, you will be able to determine how students have grown in their interests and attitudes toward reading. You will be able to determine the extent to which your independent reading program has had an impact on your students' growth as readers.

MONITORING INDEPENDENT READING

Determining whether students are engaging in independent reading during time reserved for it is a major concern. Often students engage in what we call "fake" reading during independent or sustained silent reading time. As a result, students may not become significantly more proficient in reading despite the time invested in independent reading.

Time in learning is precious, and if students are expected to engage in independent reading in school or at home they need to be made accountable for that time. To promote accountability you can monitor the time students actually spend in reading and what they do during that time. To that end, we feel that a simple monthly or weekly logsheet, located in each student's journal would help you (and your students) track students' independent reading. Figure 7.2 presents one example of a personal logsheet that students (or their teachers or parents at home) can easily use.

The form is a constant reminder for students that they are responsible for the time they spend in independent reading, whether at home or in school. Moreover, it forces students to respond to their reading and what they have read by estimating their own level of engagement and providing a comment or two. For you, the form provides data you can use to track students' actual reading over time, note trends in time and engagement, and study the extent to which independent

Name _____

Month _____

Day	Title of book	Time begun independent reading	Time stopped independent reading	Minutes in independent reading	Level of engagement in reading 1 = High 5 = Low	Comments about reading
1						
2						
3						
4						
5						
6						
7						
8						
9						
10						
11						
12						
13						
14						
15						
16						

17						
18						
19						
20						
21						
22						
23						
24						
25						
26						
27						
28						
29						
30						
31						

FIGURE 7.2. Monthly independent reading logsheet.

reading is associated with growth over time—students who read the most should experience the greatest gains in reading achievement over the course of the school year.

Forms such as these can easily be adapted to gain other types of information about students' reading—from type of materials students read to their level of satisfaction with independent reading, to times of the year or day in which independent reading seems to be most productive.

ASSESSING GROWTH OVER TIME AND PROFICIENCY IN VARIOUS ELEMENTS OF READING

In the previous chapter, we noted several specific areas of reading that are essential to overall reading growth. Independent reading can play an important role in fostering growth in these areas. In order to employ independent reading for these other purposes, it is important to identify students who can benefit from targeted instruction and independent reading activities. Authentic reading, in the form of informal reading assessments, informal reading inventories (Johnson, Kress, & Pikulski, 1987; Pikulski, 1990), or curriculum-based reading measurements (Deno, 1985) can be used to assess several of these important areas.

Word Recognition

The ability to read words accurately is key to success in reading. However, how can you know if a student is sufficiently proficient in word recognition or needs particular assistance in this area? Fortunately, a long tradition of research into informal reading assessment (Deno, 1997; Deno, Mirkin, & Chiang, 1982; Fuchs & Fuchs, 1986; Fuchs, Deno, & Mirkin, 1984; Fuchs, Fuchs, & Deno, 1982; Fuchs, Fuchs, & Maxwell, 1988; Johnson et al., 1982; Pikulski, 1990; Rasinski, 2004) allows teachers to easily assess word recognition during authentic oral reading. Moreover, this approach to informal word recognition assessment has become ubiquitous through the various forms of informal reading inventories that have been published over the past several decades (e.g., Rasinski & Padak, 2005a, 2005b).

In order to assess word recognition, ask a student to read a grade-level passage of 100–200 words orally. The passage can come from trade books or instructional materials (e.g., a basal reader) that is written at grade level. During the student's oral reading of the passage, follow along silently and mark any uncorrected error that the student makes during the reading. Any uncorrected mispronunciation, substitution, word reversal, omission, insertion, or word that is not attempted but that you supply is counted as an error.

Because some students may be unnerved at the sight of you monitoring and marking any errors during their reading, you may want to audio record the student's reading. Later, when the student is not present, you can score the student's reading.

Once the marking is completed, determine the percentage of words that were read correctly on the grade-level passage. This can be calculated by dividing the number of words read correctly by the total number of words read. For example, if a student reads a passage of 147 words in length and makes 7 errors during the reading, the percentage of words read correctly is determined by dividing 140 (147 minus 7 errors) by 147 total words. This results in a word recognition score of 95.2% of the words read correctly.

Once the word recognition score is determined, the teacher can interpret the score by referring to Table 7.1. Scores below 93% indicate that the student's word recognition is not where it should be on grade-level material. A student reading below 93% in word recognition would benefit from direct instruction in decoding words and in independent reading opportunities that are aimed at improving word recognition.

This word recognition assessment is simple and quick. We recommend that when you assess students in this way, you have students read two or three passages and average the scores.

Done at the beginning of the school year, this word recognition

TABLE 7.1. Word Recognition Scores

Score range	Reading level
98–100%	Independent reading level (outstanding)
93–97%	Instructional reading level (satisfactory)
< 93%	Frustration reading level (unsatisfactory)

assessment can identify those students who are having difficulty in word recognition. It can also help you identify the level of reading material that is most appropriate for your students. Those students who score below 93% on grade level material would benefit from reading material that is easier than grade placement. Students who score at the independent level could read material at or even slightly above their grade placement.

Because this word recognition assessment is so quick and simple, you can administer it several times throughout the school year. By administering the assessment every 2 or 3 months, you will be able to determine whether your instruction is having an effect on students' word recognition—students should demonstrate improved word recognition over time. If improvement is not noted, you may want to adjust your instruction appropriately, seek assistance and guidance from the reading specialist or coach, or refer the students for additional types of instructional intervention.

Reading Fluency–Automaticity

Automaticity is that part of reading fluency that takes word recognition to the next level. Not only is it important for students to read words accurately, they need to read words effortlessly or automatically so that they can devote the maximum amount of their cognitive energy to comprehending the written text.

Automaticity is normally measured by measuring how fast students read—their reading rate. Readers who read at a faster clip are generally thought to be reading the words at a more automatic level—effortless reading of words correlates with faster reading. The same informal method for assessing word recognition can also be employed for assessing automaticity.

In the informal reading assessment described earlier, students orally read a passage written at the assigned grade level. Word recognition errors are marked and the percentage of words read correctly is determined. For automaticity, you will simply need to determine the last word the student has read at the end of the first minute of reading. Then, when you are scoring word recognition, you also count the number of words that the student read correctly in that first minute. This words-correct-per-minute score is compared with the 50th percentile norms for the appropriate grade and time of year in Table 7.2.

Students who score significantly below these norms should be considered at-risk in the area of automaticity and should be provided with instruction that aims to improve automaticity. Independent reading should also be structured to help students improve the automaticity component of their reading fluency.

As with word recognition, this assessment can be done early in the year to get benchmark data and identify students with particular reading needs. It can also be administered regularly throughout the year to determine if students are making progress in automaticity.

When administering the assessment for word recognition and fluency, you want to obtain valid results; therefore, remind students to read in their normal voices and not to try to read as quickly as they can. The norms in Table 7.2 are based on students reading in their normal, most authentic manner.

Using reading rate as a measure of one aspect of reading has the potential for giving students an incorrect idea of reading. From regular assessments of reading rate, some students (and teachers, for that matter) may acquire the notion that reading rate and proficient reading are one and the same. This, of course, is an incorrect conception of proficient reading. So, students need to be reminded periodically that although reading rate is a way to assess one aspect of reading,

TABLE 7.2. 50th Percentile Norms for Reading Rate (Words Correct per Minute)

Grade	Fall	Winter	Spring
1	05	25	50
2	50	75	90
3	75	90	105
4	95	110	125
5	110	125	140
6	125	135	150
7	130	140	155
8	135	145	160

Note. Based on EdFormation (2003).

reading as fast as possible is not an appropriate goal for reading practice or instruction.

Reading Fluency–Prosody

Prosody is that part of fluency that refers to the expressive or tonal
quality of oral reading. Readers who read with prosody use their
voices to convey meaning to themselves and any listeners. Intonation, volume, pacing, pausing, phrasing, and emphasis are among the
features of prosody. Prosodic reading requires a reader to attend to
meaning and allows the reader to make meaning that goes beyond the
words themselves. In a sense, prosody is a link between word recognition and reading comprehension. Proficient readers tend to read with
high levels of prosody.

The beauty of the informal reading assessment we have described
for assessing word recognition and automaticity is that it can be used
to assess a wide range of reading competencies—and prosody is one.
To assess prosody, simply listen to the student read a passage orally
(the same passage used for the word recognition and automaticity
assessment) and ask yourself if the reading sounds like authentic language. The prosody rubric (see Figure 7.3) may assist you (Rasinski
& Padak, 2005a, 2005b; Zutell & Rasinski, 1991).

The rubric is divided into four distinct components of prosody
and the scores for each component range from 1 to 4. The lowest
possible score overall is 4, and the highest is 16. Because the informal
reading assessment can be used to assess multiple competencies, we
recommend that you record each student's reading and at later time,
with the student not present, assess each student's oral reading for
word recognition accuracy, automaticity, and prosody. In assessing
students reading in this way, you will have the ability to examine the
reading more than once and reflect on various aspects of the reading
without feeling that you have to make an on-the-spot decision. Later,
you can examine the recorded reading with the student individually
to help the student see for him- or herself the strengths and concerns
you have noted in their reading.

In scoring prosodic reading, students rated in the lower range of
the rubric (scores of 4–8) may be considered to read with inadequate
prosody. These students should be considered for both direct instruc-

Use the following scales to rate reader fluency on the dimensions of expression and volume, phrasing, smoothness, and pace.

A. Expression and Volume
1. Reads with little expression or enthusiasm in voice. Reads words as if simply to get them out. Little sense of trying to make text sound like natural language. Tends to read in a quiet voice.
2. Some expression. Begins to use voice to make text sound like natural language in some areas of the text, but not others. Focus remains largely on saying the words. Still reads in a voice that is quiet.
3. Sounds like natural language throughout the better part of the passage. Occasionally slips into expressionless reading. Voice volume is generally appropriate throughout the text.
4. Reads with good expression and enthusiasm throughout the text. Sounds like natural language. The reader is able to vary expression and volume to match his/her interpretation of the passage.

B. Phrasing
1. Monotonic with little sense of phrase boundaries, frequent word-by-word reading.
2. Frequent two- and three-word phrases giving the impression of choppy reading; improper stress and intonation that fail to mark ends of sentences and clauses.
3. Mixture of run-ons, midsentence pauses for breath, and possibly some choppiness; reasonable stress/intonation.
4. Generally well-phrased, mostly in clause and sentence units, with adequate attention to expression.

C. Smoothness
1. Frequent extended pauses, hesitations, false starts, sound-outs, repetitions, and/or multiple attempts.
2. Several "rough spots" in text where extended pauses, hesitations, and so forth are more frequent and disruptive.
3. Occasional breaks in smoothness caused by difficulties with specific words and/or structures.
4. Generally smooth reading with some breaks, but word and structure difficulties are resolved quickly, usually through self-correction.

D. Pace (during sections of minimal disruption)
1. Slow and laborious.
2. Moderately slow.
3. Uneven mixture of fast and slow reading.
4. Consistently conversational.

Scores range from 4 to 16. Generally, scores below 8 indicate that fluency may be a concern. Scores of 8 or above indicate that the student is making good progress in fluency.

FIGURE 7.3. Multidimensional fluency rubric. Based on Zutell and Rasinski (1991).

tion and independent reading activities that are aimed at improving the prosodic reading component of reading fluency. At regular intervals, prosody can be assessed to determine if students have made improvements in this area of reading.

Vocabulary

Vocabulary refers to knowing the direct and implied meaning of words in texts that students read. Clearly, a good vocabulary is essential to proficient reading. Again, this can be assessed through the informal reading assessment described earlier. Vocabulary assessment should come after the students have orally read the grade-level passage.

After the reading is complete, simply choose five to ten words that you think are grade-level appropriate from the passage just read. Present the words to the student and ask the student to provide the meaning for the word, especially as it is used in the context of the passage. You can score each word as being fully understood (full credit), partially understood (half credit), or not sufficiently understood (no credit). If the student gives a partial response to a word, you can prompt the student to provide more information. You can also provide the word and the sentence in which it appears.

In William Steig's book *Caleb and Kate*, for example, words such as *hoddy-doddy*, *cantankerous*, *odious*, *pondering*, and *mischief* appear in the first few pages. These would be excellent choices to present to a student who had just read that portion of the book.

Determine the percentage score for the student based on the number of words fully or partially defined correctly. For example, in *Caleb and Kate*, a student who received full credit for *hoddy-doddy*, *odious*, and *mischief*, partial credit for *pondering*, and no credit for *cantankerous*, would have a percentage score of 70% (3.5/5). Scores of 70% or better indicate adequate vocabulary knowledge for passage; scores below 70% indicate that vocabulary may be a concern. Direct instruction and independent reading activities aimed at improving vocabulary would be appropriate for students experiencing difficulty in vocabulary.

As we have mentioned earlier, the vocabulary assessment can be given over more than one passage at a time to get a more robust, reliable, and valid measure of vocabulary. It can also be given throughout the school year to determine if students are making progress in their vocabulary knowledge.

Comprehension

Comprehension, of course, is the goal of reading, whether during direct instruction or during independent reading. We want students to take meaning from what they read. As with the other reading competencies we have discussed in this chapter, comprehension can be assessed simply and quickly using the very same authentic reading task we have previously used to assess word recognition, fluency, and vocabulary.

Comprehension is best assessed after the student has read a passage. So, once a student has completed reading the passage that is part of the informal reading assessment, simply ask the student to recall all that he or she can remember from reading the text. What a reader can recall is evidence of what he or she understood. The quality of the retelling can be used to assess the quality of the student's comprehension. To aid you in making an informed assessment of each student's retelling, you can employ a rubric (Rasinski & Padak, 2005a, 2005b) to guide the assessment (see Figure 7.4).

In using retelling and the rubric, tell the student prior to the reading that you are going to be asking him or her to recall when the reading is concluded. This will prompt the reader to pay attention to the meaning of the reading passage. Once the reading is complete, cover or remove the passage from the student's sight and ask what the student can remember from the passage. If the student is a bit reticent or provides what you believe is an incomplete response, you can gently prompt the student to elaborate on particular points from the passage.

Once the retelling is complete, use your best professional judgment to rate the overall quality of the recall. If the student is able to recall very little from the passage, and what is recalled seems to be random information from the passage, the student would receive a score of one or two. Scores of one or two indicate that the student struggled with making meaning and that the grade-level difficulty of the passage read is most likely at the student's frustration level.

If the student provides a retelling that captures the main idea of

1. No recall or minimal recall of only a fact of two from the passage.
2. Student recalls a number of unrelated facts of varied importance.
3. Student recalls the main idea of the passage with a few supporting details.
4. Student recalls the main idea along with a fairly robust set of supporting details, although not necessarily organized logically or sequentially as presented in the passage.
5. Student recall is a comprehensive summary of the passage, presented in a logical order and/or with a robust set of details, and includes a statement of main idea.
6. Student recall is a comprehensive summary of the passage, presented in a logical order and/or with a robust set of details, and includes a statement of main idea. Student also makes reasonable connections beyond the text to his/her own personal life, another text, and so forth.

FIGURE 7.4. Comprehension retelling rubric.

---

the passage and is supported by some of the detail from the passage, a score of three or four is most appropriate. Instructional reading level is reflected in scores of three or four. That is, if you would rate a student three or four on a particular passage, the grade-level difficulty of the passage is at the student's instructional level, the level at which they are able to read but require some assistance from a teacher or guide.

And, if the student can provide a comprehensive summary of the passage that includes the main idea, nearly all the supporting detail, and may even extend to connecting the content to the student's own life or something beyond the text itself, a score of five or six would most likely be assigned. Scores of five or six reflect independent-level reading, the level at which a student could read a passage successfully and without instructional support. The independent-reading level, and all levels below it, are the levels that are best suited for students' independent reading.

This method for assessing comprehension is simple and quick. It may help identify those students who may need a more thorough reading assessment. For our purposes, however, it will help identify the levels of reading most appropriate for students' independent reading in a classroom. It may also identify areas of particular need that may be addressed through direct instruction and the informed use of independent reading. Conducted several times over the course of the school year, this assessment will help you determine students' growth in reading due to instruction and student independent reading.

This book is about independent reading—how teachers can nurture academic growth and a great love for reading at the same time by creating in their classrooms opportunities for free and independent reading. When students read material of their own choosing and for their own purposes they will grow as readers—in their skill and proficiency in reading, and in their desire to engage in reading as a life-long activity. The notion of assessment may seem a bit antithetical to independent reading. Assessment may seem best when tied to issues of direct instruction—so that teachers can aim their instruction at the students' needs and monitor their growth over time.

However, in this chapter, we hope we have made the case for assessment in independent reading. Independent reading implies freedom for students to read on their own, and to read material of their own choosing for their own purposes. When independent reading is a part of the regular school curriculum, as we hope it is in all schools across the country, then both you and your students must be held accountable for the time given over to independent reading. You can make best use of independent reading when you know students' reading levels and reading interests. With this information, you can stock the classroom with reading materials that students can read and want to read, making it most likely that students will find material that they will read successfully, find the independent reading experience satisfying, and grow as readers.

Further, when you are aware of students' strengths and weaknesses in reading, you can create response and other activities, drawn from and based on independent reading, that help students overcome whatever weaknesses they may have in reading. Students who need extra practice in fluency, for example, might be asked to find a particularly interesting portion of a book and prepare an oral rendition of it. Those who need comprehension assistance might be asked to create a story map. Assessment can also help you determine if these activities are having the intended impact on students' reading problems. For their part, students need to provide you with evidence that they are spending the time allotted for independent reading actually engaged in reading.

In this chapter, we have provided you with simple, quick, and valid methods for assessing and monitoring these important issues related to independent reading. When you make independent reading satisfying for your students and can determine the results of independent reading, students are most likely to validate their own efforts in independent reading and be inspired to continue and enhance this critical portion of their reading curriculum.

CHAPTER 8

Family Literacy

Reading Together at Home

Family literacy emphasizes the importance of parental involvement in children's education. The field of emergent and elementary literacy values parents as a child's first teacher and focuses on the potential of home literacy involvement to improve children's learning. Children who acquire successful reading skills are likely to have more positive school experiences (Senechal & LeFevre, 2002) and tend to remain good readers. Conversely, children who experience difficulty in learning to read continue to struggle throughout their school years (Roberts, Jurgens, & Burchinal, 2005). Purcell-Gates (1996) indicates that, through the first grade, the family's influence on children's school achievement is at least as strong as the school's.

The benefits of reading together at home are clear, and there is much that teachers can do to support home literacy involvement. It is important for teachers to understand that by working with families, children can be better prepared to meet academic goals and to develop a lifelong interest in reading (Crawford & Zygouris-Coe, 2006). Unfortunately, programs for prospective teachers typically provide student teachers with limited information about establishing home–school connections and limited supervised experiences working with families (International Reading Association, 2002). The purpose of this chapter is to illuminate the importance of home literacy and to present suggestions for its effective implementation.

LITERACY AT HOME: WHY DOES IT MATTER?

The importance of parental involvement in children's early reading is widely recognized by researchers and practitioners. Children whose families encourage reading at home have higher phonemic awareness and decoding skills (Burgess, 1999), higher reading achievement in the elementary grades (Cooter, Marrin, & Mills-House, 1999), and advanced oral language development (Senechal, LeFevre, & Thomas, 1998). The most important predictors of children's reading success have been found to be the following (Snow et al., 1998):

1. The value placed on literacy in the home.
2. Time spent reading with children.
3. The availability and use of reading materials.

HOW CAN AN EFFECTIVE HOME LITERACY ENVIRONMENT BE DEVELOPED?

Parents can seek to create a print-rich environment in the home. Having a variety of books, magazines, comic books, and newspapers available for joint or individual exploration is a start. For example, many children enjoy reading nonfiction; magazines, newspapers, and nonfiction texts can provide opportunities to explore real-life topics and concepts.

In *Literacy Tips for Children*, Mraz, Padak, and Baycich (2002) offer suggestions to parents on what they should look for at different stages in a child's early literacy development, how to support literacy development at each stage, and what reading materials are appealing to children at different developmental levels.

During the prekindergarten and kindergarten years (from ages 4 to 6) parents should look for their child to do the following:

- Show an interest in books; ask to be read to.
- Have favorite books or favorite authors; these are stories that their child may want to read, or have read to them, again and again.

- Ask questions and make comments about stories; connect stories to personal experiences.
- Pretend to read.
- Begin to understand concepts of print (see Figure 8.1).
- Learn the alphabet.
- Learn the sounds that correspond to letters of the alphabet.
- Learn how to rhyme.
- Scribble or pretend to write. Throughout kindergarten, the child should begin to write with an increasing degree of accurate sound–letter correspondence. For example, *book* might be written as B or BK.

During these early years, parents can help their child to development his or her literacy skills by doing the following:

- Point out print in their child's environment, such as print on food labels, in restaurants, on toys, while riding in a car.
- Sing songs and recite nursery rhymes or short poems; play rhyming games (see Figure 8.2 for suggestions).
- Read aloud together.

- Print is read from left to right.
- The end of a line of print does not necessarily signify the end of a thought or the end of a sentence.
- The concepts of *first* and *last*; for example, being able to point to the first letter and the last letter in a word.
- The concept of a letter.
- The concept of a word.
- The difference between the front and the back of the book, as well as the top and the bottom.
- How to correctly turn the pages of a book.
- The difference between print and pictures.
- That pictures on a page are related to the message in the printed words.
- Where to begin reading on a page.
- What a title is.
- What an author does.
- What an illustrator does.

FIGURE 8.1. Concepts of print. Based on Cunningham (2000) and Morrow (2005).

Avni, F.–"Fiddle Around with the Middle Sound"
Bethie.–*Really Silly Songs about Animals*
Bollinger, C.–"Let's Make a Rhyme"
Dines, K.–"Oodles and Oodles of Noodles"
Guthrie, W.–*Song to Grow On*
Palmer, H.–"Bounce!"
Raffi–*The Raffi Singable Songbook*
Whitfield, G.–"Apples and Bananas"
"Do–Re–Mi" ("Doe, a Deer")
"Hickory Dickory Dock"
"Mary Had a Little Lamb"
"Row, Row, Row Your Boat"
"Sing a Song of Sixpence"
"Three Blind Mice"
"Twinkle, Twinkle Little Star"

FIGURE 8.2. Children's songs for rhyming and phonemic awareness.

- Encourage their child to read aloud to family members, such as an older sibling.
- Go to the library together. Utilize library programs and materials that may be available, such as interactive story times, costumes for dramatizing readings, art materials for preparing creative responses to readings, and computers for exploring information.
- Have reading materials, such as books, magazines, and newspapers available in the home.
- Let their child see them reading.
- Encourage their child to write messages by listening for the sounds that they hear in the words they wish to write. These messages can include grocery lists, postcards, or to-do lists. Model conventional spelling for children, but do not expect them to use conventional spelling in their own writing at this stage.

Books that may be helpful for early readers include:

- Stories that rhyme.
- Adventure stories or silly stories.
- Themed books that match their child's interests, such as books about animals, children, or vehicles.
- Poems.
- Stories with repetitive text.

As children gain experience with reading and progress in their literacy development, parents should look for their child to begin to do the following in the early elementary school years, around ages 7–8:

- Begin to read independently; children should gradually develop knowledge of some sight words and should be able to decipher some words by decoding them and by using context clues.
- Begin to read aloud fluently using appropriate expression, pacing, and phrasing.
- Become familiar with different types of books and genres.
- Be able to talk about what he or she has read.
- Write notes, sentences, and paragraphs that demonstrate an increasing use of conventional spelling, rather than invented spelling.

To support children's literacy development in the early elementary grades, parents can do the following:

- Talk with their child about what he or she is reading; ask questions about the books and about the child's response to these books.
- Make reading part of their own daily routine as well as part of their child's routine. Doing so will allow their child opportunities to see the adults in their life using reading consistently and for authentic purposes.
- Continue to read aloud with their child even after the child has learned to read some books independently. Encourage their child to use strategies that will help him or her to decipher difficult words. For example, if the child happens upon an unfamiliar word, the parent can encourage the child to continue reading to the end of the sentence; then the parent may ask the

child to return to the unknown word, asking, "What makes sense and looks like the word on the page?"

- Play word games, such as those suggested in Figure 8.3.
- Continue to visit the public library.

Books that may be helpful for more advanced readers include the following:

- Mystery and adventure stories.
- Informational books.
- Books that describe and illustrate how to make things.
- Books that are part of an age-appropriate series.

In addition to grade-level or age-level specific suggestions, there are general recommendations that teachers can offer to families to guide their home literacy efforts. Those recommendations include:

- Look for reading materials that relate to activities or concepts that a child enjoys, such as sports, animals, or nature. Both books and children's magazines can be used to support these interests.
- Set reasonable limits for television viewing, but recognize that some age-appropriate movies and programs, particularly those that are based on books, can serve as a catalyst for reading.
- On occasion, when viewing television, turn down the volume and engage the captioning feature so that children have access to and are encouraged to read the words on the television screen.
- Look for reading opportunities in daily routines, such as cooking, using the phone book, reading the local sports schedule in a newspaper, looking for information on the World Wide Web, reading directions for using a new toy, or reading a brochure about a place to which the family may travel. Experiences such as these provide authentic reading opportunities.
- Create a positive and supportive atmosphere for reading so that reading together is something that children look forward to doing.
- Make books and other reading materials available during tran-

Aye! Eye! I!: Talk about words that sound alike, but are spelled differently such as *knight* and *night*, *feet* and *feat*, *great* and *grate*.

Children's Play: Observe children as they jump rope, play ball, and engage in other outdoor games. Use these activities to reinforce reading skills. For example, use jump rope chants to teach rhyming.

Five Senses: What does the word *popcorn* sound like, taste like, feel like, look like, smell like?

Guess Who: Choose a character from a TV show, a story, or a real-life event and try to get the parent or the child to guess who it is from the clues provided.

I See: I see an object. Describe it. Can you guess what it is? (I see an object that is round. It is used to play games. You can throw it and bounce it. Can you guess what it is? What letter or sound does it start with?)

Oral Travel Tale: Start a story. When you stop, the next person continues. Then the next person and so on until the story is finished.

Puzzles: Crosswords, word searches, and rhyme searches provide extra practice. These word games also give the child numerous opportunities to be successful and build confidence.

Riddles: Make up riddles about letters.
           What's a pirate's favorite letter? *R*
           What do people say when they can't hear you? *A*
           What do you say when you're surprised or amazed? *G*

Rhyme Time: Find rhymes while you listen to TV shows, look through newspapers and magazines, or sing songs. Even find items around the house that rhyme. For example, "Here is a map. Can you find or do something that rhymes with map?" (cap, clap, lap, nap).

Rime Time: Rimes are sound patterns that can be used to create thousands of words; for example *ack*, *ish*, *ill*, *an*, *ug*. Try to make as many words as you can from the chosen rime such as *back*, *Jack*, *lack*, *pack*, *quack*, *rack*, *sack*, and *tack*.

Tongue Twisters: Practicing tongue twisters can help to reinforce the beginning sounds of words. Use familiar ones like "Peter Piper picked a peck of pickled peppers," or create your own: "Tim took time to talk to Tina."

FIGURE 8.3. Games that support reading.

---

sition times, such as while waiting for an appointment or on the way to a destination.

Reading Aloud with Children

Reading aloud is one of the most important experiences teachers and parents can provide for young children (Snow et al., 1998). When children listen to texts being read aloud, they can increase their knowledge of words and develop comprehension skills (National Reading Panel, 2000a). Encouraging parents to read aloud to their children can have a positive effect on children's vocabulary, reading development, and attitudes toward reading (Barbour, 1998; Bus, van IJzendoorn, & Pellegrini, 1995). Children who acquire positive attitudes toward reading are more likely to become proficient and avid readers (Bailey, 2006).

Read-alouds can be a useful technique for home reading as well. The benefits of doing so are numerous. Rasinski (2003) summarizes those benefits: In addition to building interest in reading, read-alouds help to improve comprehension and vocabulary (Beck, McKeown, & Kucan, 2001; Cohen, 1968), increase fluency (Rasinski & Padak, 2001), and build motivation for reading (Ivey & Broaddus, 2001).

The same elements that are taken into account by a teacher when preparing for a read-aloud in the classroom should be considered for home read-alouds as well: timing, atmosphere, and book selection (Rasinski, 2003). Parents will want to select a time for read-alouds during which both they and their child can focus on reading in a relaxed and comfortable manner. For this reason, bedtime is often a suitable read-aloud time in many households. The amount of time spent reading depends on the needs of the child and parent, and may vary according to schedules and to the book that is being read.

Parents should seek to establish an atmosphere for the read-aloud that is both calm and enjoyable. Curling up in a comfortable chair with a good book and a favorite stuffed toy may help a child to feel relaxed. Then, reading together is something that the child will look forward to doing.

In terms of selecting books for home read-alouds, parents should be encouraged to read a variety of different genres with their child, both fiction and nonfiction. These books may include trade books, predictable texts, fairy tales, folk tales, poetry, and biographies. Teachers may also wish to encourage parents to read books with their child that are slightly below that child's reading level or books that have become "old favorites." Doing so can help a developing reader to build confidence and fluency. Read-aloud selections should include books about topics that are of interest to the child, as well as books that allow the child to make connections to experiences in his or her own life experiences. Figure 8.4 suggest some books that are engaging

Books:
Banks, K. (1988). *Alphabet soup.* Knopf.
Brown, M. (2005). *Goodnight moon.* New York: HarperCollins.
Falwell, C. (1998). *Word wizard.* Boston: Houghton Mifflin.
Fox, M. (1987). *Hattie and the fox.* New York: Simon & Schuster.
Geisel, T. S. (Dr. Seuss). (1957). *The cat in the hat.* New York: Random House.
Geisel, T. S. (Dr. Seuss). (1960). *Green eggs and ham.* New York: Random House.
Keats, E. J. (1977). *Whistle for Willie.* New York: Puffin Books.
Lionni, L. (1963). *Swimmy.* New York: Knopf.
Martin, B. Jr. (1995). *Brown bear, brown bear, what do you see?* New York: Henry Holt.
Martin, B. Jr., & Archambault, J. (1989). *Chicka chicka boom boom.* New York: Simon & Schuster.
Viorst, J. (1972). *Alexander and the terrible, horrible, no good, very bad day.* New York: Simon & Schuster.

Book Sources:
Newbery and Caldecott Award Winners are listed, respectively, at *www.ala.org/ ala/alsc/awardsscholarships/literaryawds/newberymedal/newberywinners/ medalwinners.cfm* and *www.ala.org/ala/alsc/onwardsscholarships/ literaryawds/caldecottmedal/caldecottwinners/caldecottmedal.cfm.*
Children's Choices booklist is published annually in the October issue of *The Reading Teacher*, a publication of the International Reading Association. Teachers' Choices booklist appears in the November issue of this journal. Visit the organization's website at *www.reading.org/resources/tools/choices_ childrens.html* and *www.reading.org/resources/tools/choices_teachers.html.*

FIGURE 8.4. Suggested books and book sources for shared book reading.

for at-home read-aloud time, as well as sources for award-winning books.

Another strategy for reading aloud, which provides support to a beginning reader, is *paired reading*. Paired reading involves the parent and child reading aloud together simultaneously (Koskinen & Blum, 1986; Rasinski & Padak, 2001; Topping, 1987). As described in Chapter 4, this strategy allows the child to be supported by a more capable reader as he or she reads books that might be too difficult to read independently. The parent and child can begin paired reading by reading aloud together. Then, when the child feels comfortable reading aloud by himself or herself, he or she can signal the parent to stop reading aloud so that the child can continue reading on his or her own.

Waldbart, Meyers, and Meyers (2006) highlight some of the activities that can be implemented at home before, during, and after paired reading:

- Before reading, the child can make predictions or talk about the visuals within the text. For example, the parent might say, "Look at the pictures on the cover of the book. What do you think this story might be about?"
- During reading, the parent can point to words as they read together and ask the child about different words, letters, punctuation marks, and word patterns. For example, the parent might say, "Here's a new word. What sound do you hear at the beginning? Does it look like a word we have seen before? What is the ending sound? Let's say the word together."
- After reading, the child can demonstrate his or her understanding of the story by matching the predictions with the actual story, retelling portions of the story, or focusing on vocabulary words. For example, after reading the folktale *Hansel and Gretel*, the parent might say, "Tell me about the part about Hansel's plan to find his way out of the forest."

Building a Spoken and Listening Vocabulary

Researchers recognize that children's oral language development is an important part of both early literacy development and long-term literacy growth (Dickinson & Tabors, 2001). Young children's listening and speaking competence often precedes their reading and writing competence (Beck, McKeown, & Kucan, 2002). Helping children to build their expressive and receptive vocabularies contributes to their overall oral language development.

Children build spoken language by listening and by talking (Armbruster, Lehr, & Osborn, 2003; Strickland, Morrow, & Neuman, 2004). Consequently, children need ample opportunities to listen and to converse at home. As Armbruster et al. (2001) explained, "Children who do not hear a lot of talk and who are not encouraged to talk themselves often have problems learning to read" (p. 4). Snow et al. (1998) report a positive relationship between the amount of time an adult talks with a child and that child's literacy development. So, what can parents and children talk about? Some suggestions are offered below:

- Snow and Beals (2006) emphasize the importance of mealtime talk. They contend that "The kind of talk that normally occurs at mealtimes provides rich information to children about the meaning of words, and thus constitutes a context for learning vocabulary embedded in all the other kinds of learning that are going on" (p. 63).
- Parents and children can engage in a walk-and-talk, highlighting the sights they see and the environmental print they observe such as street signs, billboards, store signs, products in the supermarket, and so on that are prevalent in their neighborhood. A drive or ride on the bus would serve a similar purpose.
- Parents and children can talk together about what they have viewed on television or about the video games that children play. A conversation such as this can lead to creating pictures and books about words and concepts.
- Parents should encourage children to talk with them about what is happening at school, the friends they are making, favorite books they are reading, and topics or activities that interest them.
- Parents and children can create their own imaginary stories, and they can dramatize stories they have read. (See Figure 8.5 for suggestions on ways to dramatize children's literature.)

What Next? Predict what will happen next in the story and act it out.

Who Are You? Become the character or the word.

Charades: Act out the word or the character.

I Interview U: Interview a character from the story or an interesting word in the story.

Grab Bag: Select an item from a bag and create a skit about it.

Character or Vocabulary Parade: Dress up as a character or a word and have a parade around the block or around the house.

Mind Magic: Create original stories and songs and act them out.

Sing Along: Act out the lyrics to familiar songs or write the last word in each line on a card and act them out.

Puppetry: Design puppets to depict the various characters and stage a puppet show.

Finger Plays: Develop hand signs to go along with part of a story.

Prop Shop: Have a variety of props handy to do improvisations and then talk and write about them together, for example, a nurse's hat or fireman's hat.

FIGURE 8.5. Learning to read through dramatizations.

Talking to children, giving them repeated exposures to words, and providing numerous opportunities for them to talk and listen help to increase their vocabulary and ultimately impact their comprehension skills. Children raised in poverty often enter school deficient in their vocabulary development because they do not have those fre- quent conversations and exposures to words (Neuman, 2006). This factor has a pronounced impact on early reading success in school.

Like oral language development, vocabulary development also requires that students have multiple exposures to and experiences with words. There are a number of things parents can do at home to help. For example, parents and child can together create a word wall that includes the new words the child is learning, or keep a list of "cool words" on the refrigerator. Or they can compile a scrapbook soundscape together that includes pictures that represent the sounds heard at the beginning of words as well as words created from those sounds. Nonfiction sources, such as trade books, newspaper articles, magazine articles, and travel brochures are excellent resources to use to guide children's speaking and listening vocabularies (Beck et al., 2002).

Storytelling

Most children enjoy stories: They enjoy reading them, hearing them, and telling them. Storytelling has a prominent place in the home as a way of supporting children's literacy development. Storytelling is an important skill in intellectual development (Kim, 1999). Barone and Morrow (2003) explain, "The ability to engage children in a story so deeply that they adopt its literary language, explore the motivation of the characters, and try out multiple ways of being in a character's role is effective in promoting children's literacy and language growth" (pp. 157–158).

Stadler and Ward (2005) indicate that stories and narratives support children's oral language development and enhance their conceptual knowledge. At home, parents can use their own lives and experiences as a basis for storytelling. Looking through family photo albums or scrapbooks and telling stories about the people who are known to, or connected to, the child can pique a child's interest. Storytelling from sources such as these can allow the child to connect his or her own experiences to the new story. Parents can tell children their own favorite stories, fairy tales, or fables. Wordless picture books can also be used as a way to create stories from illustrations while simultaneously developing the child's imagination, critical thinking, and sequencing skills.

SUMMER READING

Teachers often lament the fact that, when students return to the classroom after the lengthy summer break, too many of them seem to have lost much of the knowledge that they had acquired at the end of the previous school year. Teachers, then, use part of each new school year trying to review and recapture that lost knowledge. Often, it is the students who can least afford to lose the reading gains they have achieved during the school year who have fallen the farthest behind. The National Assessment of Educational Progress (2005) reported that proficient readers are improving while struggling readers are continuing to lose ground.

Summer reading loss refers to the decline in children's reading development that often occurs during summer vacation times when children are away from the classroom and not participating in formal literacy programs (Allington & McGill-Franzen, 2003). Research suggests that the impact of summer reading loss on students, particularly on at-risk students, is significant.

In their review of 13 empirical studies representing approximately 400,000 students, Cooper, Nye, Charlton, Lindsay, and Greathouse (1996) found that the reading proficiency levels of students from lower-income families declined over the summer months, while the reading proficiency levels of students from middle-income families improved. This decline resulted in an estimated 3-month achievement gap between less advantaged and more advantaged students. Over the course of several school years, the potential cumulative effect of such a decline is compounded and can result in an ever widening gap in both achievement and knowledge.

Similarly, when examining 3,000 students over a 2-year period, Heynes (1987) found that students who scored in the top quartile made rapid gains during the academic year and modest gains during the summer months. The reading achievement of average students remained unchanged or fell slightly. By contrast, students who scored in the bottom quartile made slower gains in reading achievement during the academic year and then lost a significant portion of those gains over each summer. This synthesis of research suggests that summer reading loss seems to have its greatest impact on low-achieving and low-income students—those who can least afford to fall further behind.

Why does summer reading loss occur? Access to reading materials has been consistently identified as a critical element in enhancing the reading development of children. Of all the activities in which children engage outside of school, time spent actually reading is the best predictor of reading achievement: The more students read, the better readers they become (Anderson, Wilson, & Fielding, 1988).

All too often, however, struggling readers have little or no opportunity beyond the classroom to improve their reading proficiency (Coats & Taylor-Clark, 2001). Children from low-income households have a limited selection of books to read both within their homes and within their communities (McQuillan, 1998). Neuman and Celano (2001) found that middle-income communities had up to three businesses selling children's books for every one such business that existed in poorer communities. In middle-income communities, an estimated 13 books were available per individual child. In low-income communities, the availability of books was estimated to be approximately 1 book for every 300 children.

What can be done to address the problem of summer reading loss? Providing children with access to books is a start. In some schools where reading materials are not readily available in the homes of their students, grants have helped to provide books and supplies needed for home literacy learning. For example, at the start of the summer, some schools use grant funding to provide bags of books to students and their families. In addition to books, these bags can contain suggested activities and recommendations for additional reading resources.

Parents also need specific suggestions on how to participate in family literacy and on what books and resources to use, and they need to be supported in their attempts to do so (Edwards, 2004). Figure 8.6 offers some suggestions that teachers can make to families about enhancing home literacy during the summer months. The following suggestions, adapted from the work of Mraz and Rasinski (2007), are intended to help both schools and families address the problem of summer reading loss:

- Host workshops for parents before the start of summer vacation. Explain why reading with children over the summer is so important. Suggest age-appropriate books, materials, and routines that may be helpful.
- Coordinate a parent workshop with the local public library. Invite a library representative to attend the workshop and to provide library cards for interested families, as well as information on summer reading programs offered at the library.
- Send home a required summer reading list of three to five favorite titles for which children will be accountable when the new school year begins. Make sure that the assigned books are readily available at local bookstores or through the public library.

Summer Reading Projects: Provide students with a choice of books and prepare a list of creative, fun projects they can complete, such as pictures with captions, poetry, a game based on the book, character cards, a clay sculpture, a play, a symbol representing each of the main characters, a mobile, a t-shirt design, a collage, a diary.

Library Day: Encourage parents to take their children to the local library at least once a week to select books and enjoy the many activities available, such as story time.

Cultural Outings: Enjoy a day at a museum or the zoo. Talk about the excursion. Draw pictures, write poems, play word games about the trip.

Vivid Vacations: Use vacations as a source of talking and writing material.

Home Adventure: Engage in some of the activities mentioned previously that work well at home such as drama, word games, guessing games, and read-alouds. Use materials found in the home such as magazines, cereal boxes, junk mail, and newspapers to engage in fun reading activities. Take pictures of some of the activities occurring during the day and dictate or write stories about them. Use the computer, if available, to locate websites that offer lots of ideas for fun reading activities.

Neighborhood Excursions: "Walk and talk" or "ride and chat" to generate ideas to write about, draw pictures about, or investigate new words encountered during the outing.

FIGURE 8.6. Activities to enhance reading during the summer months.

- If at all possible, consider making the school library accessible on a limited basis over the summer months to facilitate student reading and access to materials.
- With the help of the school parent–teacher association, arrange a schoolwide summer reading program through which students submit weekly logs of the texts and number of minutes they read. A team of parents can tally the logs by individual student, grade level, and whole school. The school can display the cumulative total of minutes read, and students' own book reviews can be posted. The new school year could then begin with a celebration of achieving the summer reading goals, with special recognition given to individual students and grade levels who achieved or exceeded their goals.

WHAT CAN SCHOOLS DO
TO SUPPORT HOME LITERACY?

Family literacy professionals often assert that parents are their children's first and most important teachers. Yet many parents remain unfamiliar with young children's developmental progression toward proficiency as readers and writers. Other parents may want to do *something* at home to help their children succeed as emergent readers, but they are unfamiliar with exactly *what* to do to support that growth. When parents perceive a teacher to be welcoming, accessible, and responsive to their questions and concerns, a productive rapport can be established. That connection can, in turn, serve to support the child's literacy learning and development (Mraz, Padak, & Rasinski, 2008).

At the beginning of the school year, it can be helpful to hold an information-gathering conference between parents and teachers so that they have the opportunity to become acquainted with one another, to ask questions, and to gather information that can help both parties better understand the needs of the child and how best to support those needs. When a face-to-face meeting between parents and teachers is not possible, often a simple survey can help parents to communicate to the teacher important information about home reading patterns, interests, and challenges. Figure 8.7 provides an example of such a survey.

By establishing home–school communication patterns that are both consistent and positive, teachers can help parents to understand that they are an important piece of the learning-to-read puzzle. Teachers can provide parents with guidance, knowledge, and suggested materials that can be used to complement the learning that takes place at school. According to the National Center for Family Literacy (2004), parents need to know that they are valued, and they must be empowered to demonstrate to their children that learning is important by establishing an appropriate learning environment in the home.

Epstein (1995) explains, "The way schools care about children is reflected in the way schools care about the children's families" (p. 702). There are many ways for teachers and school administrators to demonstrate their support of family literacy. Some of those ways include:

What activities does your child enjoy the most at home? _____

_____

What activities does your child enjoy the least at home? _____

_____

On a scale of 1 to 10, with 10 being "reading is my child's favorite activity" and 1 being "reading is my child's least favorite activity," how would you rate the degree to which your child enjoys reading? _____

How often does your child read at home? _____

How often are you able to read with your child?_____

Do you visit the library with your child? If so, how often?_____

What type of books or other reading materials does your child like to read? _____

What do you find challenging about reading at home with your child? (Check all that apply.)
☐ Finding the time to read together.
☐ I'm not sure what books or other reading materials to select for reading at home.
☐ We don't have enough books or other reading materials to read in our home.
☐ Reading together is frustrating; it's not something we enjoy doing together.
☐ I'm not sure how to help when my child has difficulty reading.
☐ We need help reading English.
☐ Other (please list).

What information did you need to know about your local library? (Check all that apply.)
☐ The library location and hours.
☐ How to use the library.
☐ Services and programs offered at the library.
☐ Help obtaining a library card.
☐ Help in choosing appropriate books.
☐ Other (please list).

Which of the following did you find helpful for providing you with information about literacy learning?
☐ A classroom newsletter.
☐ A parent message board posted in or outside of the classroom.
☐ Personal notes from the teacher.
☐ Personal phone calls from the teacher.

FIGURE 8.7. Sample family reading survey questions for the beginning of the school year. Based on Mraz, Padak, and Rasinski (2008).

- Having an open-door policy between the home and the school. This encourages parents to visit and to ask questions or express concerns. A parent center filled with resources such as books, periodicals, games, songs and Internet sources can be a supportive and informative gathering place.
- Making available opportunities for parents to volunteer at the school by, for example, serving as a guest reader in a classroom or by assisting with the processing of monthly book orders.
- Sending home a periodic newsletter to apprise parents of the types of learning activities that are happening in the classroom and to provide additional ideas and strategies that parents can use at home.
- Establishing a website for those parents who have access to a computer can serve many of the same functions as a newsletter—to provide a synopsis of what is going on in the classroom and to suggest additional ideas and resources that can be used at home to support the learning that occurs in the classroom.
- Many family members think that their level of education precludes them from being able to help their child with schoolwork. Providing parent workshops and family literacy events can be particularly helpful when trying to increase the parent's role in the child's literacy development. These workshops can be designed to teach parents specific literacy skills, such as questioning strategies, how to scaffold the child's learning, and different ways to provide positive feedback to their child. Parenting skills such as effective discipline, proper nutrition, and ways to communicate with their child can also be incorporated into these workshops. Workshops can focus on providing materials for parents or can introduce a guest speaker who can share practical suggestions for working with children at home. A literacy event might include a book study or it might have books for sale or for borrowing. If the relationship between the school and the home becomes an important part of the culture of the educational setting, parents will not only feel welcome, but will better understand their role in the school community.
- Sending home materials that parents can use to reinforce the lessons being taught at school can be beneficial. These activities should not represent new learning, but should serve as a review

of lessons being taught during the school day. Teachers need to provide parents with specific information on how to implement these activities at home. For example, instead of simply sending home a worksheet on phonemic awareness, a teacher could ask parents to encourage their child to find items around the house that begin with a particular sound. This way, children are more likely to enjoy home literacy time as they gain practice with the concept of sound/letter correspondence.

CONCLUSION

"Literacy," according to Heath (1983), "rather than a set of skills, is a way of thinking, learned through communication with families" (cited in Thomas, Fazio, & Stiefelmeyer, 1999, p. 9). Research has demonstrated the impact of strong parental support, both at home and at school, on children's reading achievement. Creating an environment that is filled with a variety of print materials, that models the importance of reading, and that encourages children to read is a major step toward motivating young children to read and to enjoy reading. Teachers can support the development of such an environment.

In response to the question "Who benefits from family literacy?" a synthesis of research shows that at least four groups benefit: children, parents, families as units, and the larger society (Padak & Rasinski, 2003). Teachers can help to cultivate a viable partnership with families in order to improve the literacy learning for children. In doing so, everyone benefits.

Professional Development Ideas

Below we share questions and reflection points to help guide your use of independent reading in the classroom. Some points will apply more to some grade levels than others. You can use the following questions for both personal reflection and professional conversation with colleagues.

- *Rationale/beliefs/theory.* Why am I making time in my day for independent reading? What is the purpose for doing this in my classroom? How can I support or explain my decision to others? What does independent reading offer the readers in my room?
- *Frequency/length of time.* How much time will I devote to independent reading in my classroom? How often will independent reading occur? When will it occur during my day? Why?
- *Environment.* How can I make my classroom or instructional space a place where students will want to read? How do I create an ambiance for reading?
- *Classroom library.* What is the status of my classroom book collection right now? Do I have enough books? Do I have enough genres? Are the books accessible to students? Can they easily see new titles and covers? Are books labeled according to author, genre, or topic? Do I have labels on my book boxes so students don't have to guess? Can the students get to the books easily, or will I have major traffic jams? Can students see the full covers of some books or are all my books facing inward so students can only see the spines? What is my action plan for getting more books into the classroom? What are my thoughts about students reading magazines during independent reading time?
- *Student books.* Do I want to have book boxes on each table? Will

each student have his or her own book box? What kinds of books will I put in these boxes? How often will they be changed and who will change them?

• *Kinds of reading materials.* What can children read during independent reading time? Books that are mainly "just right"? Any book they want? Do they choose? Do I? Can they select anything? Do I want them to read a certain number of books a week? Do they have to try certain genres? What are the choices and what are the possibilities? Can children bring in materials from home or the public library? Is Internet reading acceptable?

• *Noise.* To whisper or not to whisper? What kind of talk do I believe is appropriate during independent reading time? Will I provide a place for students to talk with each other about a book? Can students read together? Can students listen to a book on tape during this time?

• *Movement.* Can the students move around during independent reading? Can they read on the floor, or do I need them to be at their desks?

• *My role.* What will I be doing while the students are independently reading? When I hold conferences, do I want the students to come to me? Will I go to them? How will I document what I learn from my conferences with each child? How often do I plan to meet with each child? What will I be looking for?

• *Keeping track.* How will I hold my students accountable for their reading? Do I want them to keep track of their reading? What purpose would that serve? What should they record when they read? How will this information inform my instruction and make me a better teacher for each child?

• *Grading.* What do I need to have in black and white in order to feel comfortable talking with parents, justifying a "grade," feeling like I have an understanding of what students are reading? Why?

• *Parental involvement.* How can I get parents and others (school staff, community members) involved in my independent reading program—in school and at home? What recommendations can I give to parents about selecting appropriate home reading materials? How can I address their questions about their child's reading level?

• *Current reading instruction.* What materials are currently available to use for teaching reading in my school? How does independent reading fit within school, district, and state guidelines? How can I find time for students to read independently within the guidelines of our reading philosophy? With whom might I need to talk in order to explain why I believe students need more time to read independently rather than only in a whole group setting?

• *Systemic school program.* I love independent reading. How can I help make this a schoolwide activity or program? What recommendations can I make to school administrators to encourage their support of an independent reading program? How can I learn about funding opportunities to support a schoolwide initiative?

- *Independent reading outside of school.* How can I keep independent reading going when school is not in session: during evenings, summer vacations, and breaks in the school schedule?

- *Controversial research.* How do I respond to school administrators or others who say that the National Reading Panel concluded that there is no evidence that independent silent reading improves students' reading?

References

Adams, M. J. (1990). *Beginning to read: Thinking and learning about print.* Cambridge, MA: MIT Press.

Allington, R. L. (1977). If they don't read much, how they ever gonna get good? *Journal of Reading, 21,* 57–61.

Allington, R. L. (1978, March). *Are good and poor readers taught differently? Is that why poor readers are poor readers?* Paper presented at the annual meeting of the American Educational Research Association, Toronto, Canada.

Allington, R. L. (1983a). The reading instruction provided readers of differing abilities. *Elementary School Journal, 83,* 556–561.

Allington, R. L. (1983b). Fluency: The neglected goal of the reading program. *The Reading Teacher, 36,* 556–561.

Allington, R. L. (2000). *What really matters for struggling readers: Designing research-based programs.* New York: Longman.

Allington, R. L. (2006). *What really matters for struggling readers: Designing research-based programs* (2nd ed.). Boston: Pearson.

Allington, R. L., & McGill-Franzen, A. (2003). The impact of summer loss on the reading achievement gap. *Phi Delta Kappan, 85,* 68–75.

Alvermann, D. E., & Guthrie, J. (1993). The National Research Center. In A. Sweet & J. I. Anderson (Eds.), *Reading research in the year 2000* (pp. 129–150). Hillsdale, NJ: Erlbaum.

Ambruster, B. B., Lehr, F., & Osborn, J. (2001). *Put reading first: The research building blocks for teaching children to read: Kindergarten through grade 3.* Washington, DC: National Institute for Literacy. Available online at *www.nifl.gov/partnershipforreading.*

Anderson, R. C., Wilson, P. T., & Fielding, L. G. (1988). Growth in reading and how children spend their time outside of school. *Reading Research Quarterly, 23,* 285–303.

Atwell, N. (1987). *In the middle.* Portsmouth, NH: Heinemann.

Atwell, N. (1998). *In the middle: New understandings about writing, reading, and learning* (2nd ed.). Portsmouth, NH: Heinemann.

Atwell, N. (2007). *The reading zone: How to help kids become skilled, passionate, habitual, critical readers.* New York: Scholastic.

Bailey, L. B. (2006). Examining gifted students who are economically at-risk to determine factors that influence their early reading success. *Early Childhood Education Journal, 33*(5), 307–315.

Barbour, A. C. (1998). Home literacy bags promote family involvement. *Childhood Education, 75*(2), 1–75.

Barone, D. M., & Morrow, L. M. (Eds.). (2003). *Literacy and young children: Research-based practices.* New York: Guilford Press.

Beck, I. L., McKeown, M. G., & Kucan, L. (2002). *Bringing words to life: Robust vocabulary instruction.* New York: Guilford Press.

Blachowicz, C., & Fisher, P. (2005). *Teaching vocabulary in all classrooms* (3rd ed.). New York: Prentice Hall.

Block, C., & Mangieri, J. (2002). Recreational reading: Twenty years later. *The Reading Teacher, 55*(6), 572–580.

Boulware, B., & Foley, C. (1998). Recreational reading: Choices of fourth graders. *Journal of Reading Education, 23*(2), 17–22.

Burgess, S. R. (1999). The influence of speech perception, oral language ability, the home literacy environment, and prereading knowledge on the growth of phonological sensitivity: A 1-year longitudinal study. *Reading Research Quarterly, 34,* 400–402.

Bus, A. G., van IJzendoorn, M. H., & Pellegrini, A. D. (1995). Joint book reading makes for success in learning to read: A meta-analysis on intergenerational transmission of literacy. *Review of Educational Research, 65,* 1–21.

Calkins, L. M. (2001). *The art of teaching reading.* New York: Addison-Wesley.

Coats, L. T., & Taylor-Clark, P. (2001). Finding a niche for reading: A key to improving underachievers' reading skills. *Reading Improvement, 38*(2), 70–73.

Cohen, D. (1968). The effect of literature on vocabulary and comprehension. *Elementary English, 45,* 209–213, 217.

Cooper, H., Nye, B., Charlton, K., Lindsay, J., & Greathouse, S. (1996). The effects of summer vacation on achievement test scores: A narrative and meta-analytic review. *Review of Educational Research, 66,* 227–268.

Cooter, R., Marrin, P., & Mills-House, E. (1999). Family and community involvement: The bedrock of reading success. *The Reading Teacher, 52*(8), 891–896.

Cramer, E. H., & Castle, M. (1994). *Fostering the love of reading: The affective domain in reading education.* Newark, DE: International Reading Association.

Crawford, C. A., & Zygouris-Coe, V. (2006). All in the family: Connecting home and school with family literacy. *Early Childhood Education Journal, 33*(4), 261–267.

Cullinan, B. (2000). Independent reading and school achievement. *School Library Media Research*. Retrieved February 10, 2007, from *www.ala. org/ala/aasl/aaslpubsandjournals/slmrb*.

Cunningham, A. E., & Stanovich, K. E. (1998). What reading does for the mind. *American Educator, 22,* 8–15.

Cunningham, P., & Allington, R. (1999). *Classrooms that work* (2nd ed.). New York: Longman.

Cunningham, P. M. (2000). *Phonics they use: Words for reading and writing.* New York: Addison-Wesley.

Cunningham, P. M. (2004). *Phonics they use* (4th ed.). New York: Allyn & Bacon.

Cunningham, P. M., Hall, D. P., & Sigmon, C. M. (1999). *The teacher's guide to the four blocks.* Greensboro, NC: Carson-Dellosa.

Daniels, H. (2002). *Literature circles: Voice and choice in book clubs and reading groups* (2nd ed.). Portland, ME: Stenhouse.

Deno, S. L. (1985). Curriculum-based measurement: The emerging alternative. *Exceptional Children, 52,* 219–232.

Deno, S. L. (1997). Whether thou goest ... Perspectives on progress monitoring. In J. W. Lloyd, E. J. Kameenui, & D. Chard (Eds.), *Issues in educating students with disabilities* (pp. 77–99). Mahwah, NJ: Erlbaum.

Deno, S. L., Mirkin, P., & Chiang, B. (1982). Identifying valid measures of reading. *Exceptional Children, 49,* 36–45.

Dickinson, D. K., & Tabors, P. O. (Eds.). (2001). *Beginning literacy with language.* Baltimore: Brookes.

Durkin, D. (1966). *Children who read early: Two longitudinal studies.* New York: Teachers College Press.

Eccles, J. (1983). Experiences, values, and academic behaviors. In J. T. Spence (Ed.), *Achievement and achievement motives* (pp. 75–146). San Francisco: Freeman.

Echols, L. D., West, R. F., Stanovich, K. E., & Zehr, K. S. (1996). Using children's literacy activities to predict growth in verbal cognitive skills: A longitudinal investigation. *Journal of Educational Psychology, 88,* 296–304.

Edformation. (2003). AIMSweb(tm): A Research Based Formative Assessment System, 2003. [Data file]. Retrieved September 17, 2003, from *www.edformation.com*.

Edwards, P. A. (2004). *Children's literacy development: Making it happen through school, family, and community involvement.* Boston: Allyn & Bacon.

Ehri, L. C. (2005). Learning to read words: Theory, findings, and issues. *Scientific Studies of Reading, 9,* 167–188.

Epstein, J. L. (1995). Family/school/community partnerships: Caring for the children we share. *Phi Delta Kappan, 76,* 701–712.

Fisher, B. (1995). *Thinking and learning together: Curriculum and community in a primary classroom.* Portsmouth, NH: Heinemann.

Five, C., & Dionisio, M. (1999). Instruction to meet special needs. *School Talk, 4*(2), 1–3.

Fountas, I., & Pinnell, G. (2001). *Guiding readers and writers.* Portsmouth, NH: Heinemann.

Fountas, I., & Pinnell, G. (2006). *Leveled books, K–8.* Portsmouth, NH: Heinemann.

Fox, M. (2001). *Reading magic: Why reading aloud to our children will change their lives forever.* San Diego, CA: Harcourt.

Fry, E. (1998). The most common phonograms. *The Reading Teacher, 5*(7), 620–622.

Fuchs, L. S., Deno, S. L., & Mirkin, P. (1984). The effects of frequent curriculum-based measurement and evaluation on pedagogy, student achievement, and students' awareness of learning. *American Educational Research Journal, 21,* 449–460.

Fuchs, L. S., & Fuchs, D. (1986). Effects of systematic formative evaluation: A meta-analysis. *Exceptional Children, 53,* 199–208.

Fuchs, L. S., Fuchs, D., & Deno, S. L. (1982). Reliability and validity of curriculum-based informal reading inventories. *Reading Research Quarterly, 18,* 6–26.

Fuchs, L. S., Fuchs, D., & Maxwell, L. (1988). The validity of informal measures of reading comprehension. *Remedial and Special Education, 9*(2), 20–28.

Gambrell, L. B. (2007). President's Message. Reading: Does practice make perfect? *Reading Today, 24*(6), 16.

Gambrell, L. B., Palmer, B. M., Codling, R. S., & Mazzoni, S. A. (1996). Assessing motivation to read. *The Reading Teacher, 49*(7), 518–533.

Gambrell, L. B., Wilson, R., & Gantt, W. (1981). Classroom observations of task-attending behaviors of good and poor readers. *Journal of Educational Research, 74,* 400–404.

Gaskins, I. W., Ehri, L. C., Cress, C. O., O'Hara, C., & Donnelly, K. (1996–1997). Procedures for word learning: Making discoveries about words. *The Reading Teacher, 50*(4), 312–327.

Greenwald, R., Hedges, L. V., & Laine, R. D. (1996). The effect of school resources on student achievement. *Review of Educational Research, 66*(3), 361–396.

Gunning, T. (1995). Word building: A strategic approach to the teaching of phonics. *The Reading Teacher, 48*(6), 484–488.

Hart, B., & Risley, T. R. (2003). The early catastrophe: The 30 million word gap by age 3. *American Educator, 27*(1), 4–9.

Hendrick, W. B., & Cunningham, J. W. (2002). Investigating the effect of wide reading on listening comprehension of written language. *Reading Psychology, 23,* 107–126.

Heynes, B. (1987). Schooling and cognitive development: Is there a season for learning? *Child Development, 55*(3), 6–10.

Hoffman, J., Sailors, M., Duffy, G., & Beretvas, S. (2004). The effective elementary classroom literacy environment: Examining the validity of the TEX-IN3 observation system. *Journal of Literacy Research, 36,* 303–334.

International Reading Association. (1999). *Resolution: On books and other print materials for classroom and school library media centers in the U.S.* Retrieved July 29, 2007, from *reading.org/downloads/resolutions/ resolution99_books_for_classrooms.pdf.*

International Reading Association. (2000). *Providing books and other print materials for classroom and school libraries: A position statement of the International Reading Association.* Newark, DE: Author.

International Reading Association. (2002). *Family–school partnerships: Essential elements of literacy instruction in the United States.* Newark, DE: Author.

Ivy, G., & Broaddus, K. (2001). "Just plain reading": A survey of what makes students want to read in middle school. *Reading Research Quarterly, 36,* 350–377.

Jewell, T., & Pratt, D. (1999). Literature discussions in the primary grades: Children's thoughtful discourse about books and what teachers can do to make it happen. *The Reading Teacher, 52*(8), 842–850.

Johnson, M. S., Kress, R. A., & Pikulski, J. J. (1987). *Informal reading inventories.* Newark, DE: International Reading Association.

Jones, C. F. (1994). *Mistakes that worked: 40 familiar inventions and how they came to be.* New York: Doubleday.

Jones, C. F. (1998). *Accidents may happen: Fifty inventions discovered by mistake.* New York: Delacorte.

Jones, C. F. (2000). *Eat your words: A fascinating look at the language of food.* New York: Delacorte.

Kim, S. (1999). The effects of storytelling and pretend play on cognitive processes, short-term and long-term narrative recall. *Child Study Journal, 29*(3), 175–185.

Koskinen, P. S., & Blum, I. H. (1986). Paired repeated reading: A classroom strategy for developing fluent reading. *The Reading Teacher, 40*(1), 70–75.

Kragler, S. (2000). Choosing books for reading: An analysis of three types of readers. *Journal of Research in Childhood Education, 14*(2), 133–141.

Krashen, S. (1993a). *The power of reading: Insights from research.* Englewood, CO: Libraries Unlimited.

Krashen, S. (1993b). The case for free voluntary reading. *Canadian Modern Language Review, 50*(1), 72–82.

Krashen, S. (2004a). *The power of reading: Insights from the research* (2nd ed.). Portsmouth, NH: Heinemann.

Krashen, S. (2004b). False claims about literacy development. *Educational Leadership, 61*(6), 18–21.

Krashen, S. (2005). Is in-school free reading good for children? *Phi Delta Kappan, 86,* 444–447.

Lewis, M., & Samuels, S. J. (2005). *Read more, read better? A meta-analysis of the literature on the relationship between exposure to reading and reading achievement.* Unpublished manuscript, University of Minnesota, Minneapolis.

Lewis, M. S. (2002). Read more—read better? A meta-analysis of the literature on the relationship between exposure to reading and reading achievement. *Dissertation Abstracts International, 63*(11), 3897.

Loughlin, C., & Ivener, B. (1987). *Literacy behaviors of kindergarten-primary children in high-stimulus literacy environments.* (ERIC Document Reproduction Service No. ED354077).

Lowe, J. (2005). *Creating an A+++ classroom library.* Retrieved July 30, 2007, from *content.scholastic.com.*

Manning, G., & Manning, M. (1984). What models of recreational reading make a difference? *Reading World, 23*(4), 375–380.

Mathewson, G. C. (1994). Model of attitude influence upon reading and learning to read. In R. B. Ruddle, M. R. Ruddle, & H. Singer (Eds.), *Theoretical models and processes of reading* (pp. 1431–1461). Newark, DE: International Reading Association.

McMahon, S., & Raphael, T. (1997). *The book club connection: Literacy learning and classroom talk.* New York: Teachers College Press.

McQuillan, J. (1998). *The literacy crisis: False claims, real solutions.* Portsmouth, NH: Heinemann.

Mooney, M. E. (1990). *Reading to, with, and by children.* Katonah, NY: Richard C. Owen Press.

Morrow, L. (2001). *Literacy development in the early years: Helping children read and write.* Needham Heights, MA: Allyn and Bacon.

Morrow, L., Tracey, D., Woo, D., & Pressley, M. (1999). Characteristics of exemplary first-grade literacy instruction. *The Reading Teacher, 52*(5), 462–476.

Morrow, L., & Weinstein, C. (1986). Encouraging voluntary reading: The impact of a literature program on children's use of library centers. *Reading Research Quarterly, 21,* 330–346.

Mraz, M., Padak, N., & Baycich, D. (2002). Literacy tips for children. *Ohio Literacy Resource Center.* Retrieved January 18, 2007, from *literacy. kent.edu/Oasis/Pubs/child_lit_tips.pdf.*

Mraz, M., Padak, N., & Rasinski, T. (2007). *Evidence-based instruction in reading: A professional development guide to phonemic awareness.* New York: Allyn & Bacon.

Mraz, M., & Rasinski, T. (2007). Summer reading loss. *The Reading Teacher, 60*(8), 784–789.

Nagy, W. E., & Anderson, R. C. (1984). How many words are there in printed school English? *Reading Research Quarterly, 19,* 304–330.

National Assessment of Educational Progress. (2002). *NAEP reading: National trends in reading.* Washington, DC: National Center for Educational Statistics.

National Assessment of Educational Progress. (2005). *Reading: The nation's report card.* Retrieved August 16, 2005, from *nces.ed.gov/nationsre-portcard/reading.*

National Center for Family Literacy. (2002). *Family literacy: A strategy for educational improvement.* Louisville, KY: National Governors Association. Retrieved November 9, 2007, from *www/nga.org/cda/files/110802LITERACY.pdf.*

National Center for Family Literacy (2004). *Report of the National Early Literacy Panel.* Washington DC: National Institute for Literacy.

National Reading Panel. (2000a). *Report of the National Reading Panel: Teaching children to read. Report of the subgroups* (NIH Publication No. 00-4754). Washington, DC: U.S. Department of Health and Human Services.

National Reading Panel. (2000b). *Teaching children to read: An evidence-based assessment of the scientific research literature on reading and its implications for reading instruction* (NIH Publication No. 00-4769). Washington, DC: national Institute of Child Health and Human Development.

Neuman, S. B. (2006). The knowledge gap: Implications for early education. In D. K. Dickinson & S. B. Neuman (Eds.), *Handbook of early literacy research* (Vol. 2, pp. 29–40). New York: Guilford Press.

Neuman, S. B., & Celano, D. (2001). Access to print in low-income and middle-income communities. *Reading Research Quarterly, 36*(1), 8–26.

No Child Left Behind Act of 2001, Pub. L. No. 107-110, 115 Stat. 1425, 20 U.S.C. §§ 6301 et seq. (2002).

Noe, K., & Johnson, N. (1999). *Getting started with literature circles.* Norwood, MA: Christopher Gordon.

Padak, N., & Rasinski, T. (2003). Family literacy programs: Who benefits? Kent, OH: Ohio Literacy Resource Center. Retrieved November 30, 2007, from *literacy.kent.edu/Oasis/Pubs/WhoBenefits2003.pdf.*

Padak, N., & Rasinski, T. (2008). *Evidence-based instruction in reading: A professional development guide for fluency instruction.* Boston: Allyn & Bacon.

Palmer, B., Codling, R., & Gambrell, L. (1994). In their own words: What elementary students have to say about motivation to read. *The Reading Teacher, 48*(2), 176–178.

Paris, S. G., & Oka, E. R. (1986). Self-regulated learning among exceptional children. *Exceptional Children, 53,* 103–108.

Pikulski, J. J. (1990). Informal reading inventories. *The Reading Teacher, 11*(7), 514–516.

Postlethwaite, T., & Ross, K. (1992). *Effective schools in reading: Implications for educational planners.* The Hague: International Association for the Evaluation of Educational Achievement.

Pressley, M., Rankin, T., & Yokoi, L. (1996). A survey of instructional practices of primary teachers nominated as effective in promoting literacy. *Elementary School Journal, 96,* 363–384.

Purcell-Gates, V. (1996). Stories, coupons, and the TV guide: Relationships between home literacy experiences and emergent literacy knowledge. *Reading Research Quarterly, 31*, 402–428.

Rasinski, T. V. (1988). The role of interest, purpose, and choice in early literacy. *The Reading Teacher, 41*(4), 396–400.

Rasinski, T. V. (2003). *The fluent reader: Oral reading strategies for building word recognition, fluency, and comprehension.* New York: Scholastic.

Rasinski, T. V. (2004). *Assessing reading fluency.* Honolulu, HI: Pacific Resources for Education and Learning.

Rasinski, T. V., & Hoffman, J. V. (2003). Theory and research into practice: Oral reading in the school literacy curriculum. *Reading Research Quarterly, 38*, 510–522.

Rasinski, T. V., & Padak, N. D. (1998). How elementary students referred for compensatory reading instruction perform on school-based measures of word recognition, fluency, and comprehension. *Reading Psychology: An International Quarterly, 19*, 185–216.

Rasinski, T. V., & Padak, N. D. (2001). *From phonics to fluency: Effective teaching of decoding and reading fluency in the elementary school.* New York: Addison Wesley Longman.

Rasinski, T. V., & Padak, N. D. (2004). *Effective reading strategies* (3rd ed.). Upper Saddle River, NJ: Prentice Hall.

Rasinski, T. V., & Padak, N. D. (2005a). *Three minute reading assessments: Word recognition, fluency, and comprehension for grades 1–4.* New York: Scholastic.

Rasinski, T. V., & Padak, N.D. (2005b). *Three minute reading assessments: Word recognition, fluency, and comprehension for grades 5–8.* New York: Scholastic.

Rasinski, T. V., & Padak, N.D. (2007). *Evidence-based instruction in reading: A progressional development guide to comprehension..* New York: Pearson/Allyn and Bacon.

Roberts, J., Jurgens, J., & Burchinal, M. (2005). The role of home literacy practices in preschool children's language and emergent literacy skills. *Journal of Speech, Language, and Hearing Research, 48*, 345–359.

Routman, R. (2003). *Reading essentials: The specifics you need to teach reading well.* Portsmouth, NH: Heinemann.

Samuels, S. J. (1979). The method of repeated readings. *The Reading Teacher, 32*(4), 403–408.

Samuels, S. J., & Wu, Y. C. (2007). *How the amount of time spent on independent reading affects reading achievement.* Unpublished manuscript.

Segel, E. (1990). Side by side storybook reading for every child: An impossible dream? *New Advocate, 3*(2), 131–137.

Senechal, M., & LeFevre, J. (2002). Parental involvement in the development of children's reading skill: A five-year longitudinal study. *Child Development, 73*, 445–460.

Senechal, M., LeFevre, J., Thomas, E., & Daley, K. E. (1998). Differential effects of home literacy experiences on the development of oral and written language. *Reading Research Quarterly, 33*(1), 96–116.

Share, D. L. (1995). Phonological recoding and self-teaching: *Sine qua non* of reading acquisition. *Cognition, 55* (1), 151–218.

Smith, F. (1988). *Joining the literacy club: Further essays into education.* Portsmouth, NH: Heinemann.

Snow, C. E., Barnes, W., Chandler, J., Goodman, I., & Hemphill, L. (1991). *Unfulfilled expectations: Home and school influences on literacy.* Cambridge, MA: Harvard University Press.

Snow, C. E., & Beals, D. E. (2006). Mealtime talk that supports literacy development. *New Directions for Child and Adolescent Development, 111,* 51–66.

Snow, C. E., Burns, M. S., & Griffin, P. (Eds.). (1998). *Preventing reading difficulties in young children.* Washington, DC: National Academy Press.

Stadler, M. A., & Ward, G. C. (2005). Supporting the narrative development of young children. *Early Childhood Education Journal, 33*(2), 73–80.

Stanovich, K. E., & West, R. F. (1989). Exposure to print and orthographic processing. *Reading Research Quarterly, 24,* 402–433.

Strickland, D. S., Morrow, L. M., & Neuman, S. B. (2004). The role of literacy in early childhood education. *The Reading Teacher, 58*(1), 86–100.

Taberski, S. (2001). *On solid ground: Strategies for teaching reading K–3.* Portsmouth, NH: Heinemann.

Taylor, B., Frye, M., & Maruyama, K. (1990). Time spent reading and reading growth. *American Educational Research Journal, 27,* 351–362.

Taylor, B., Pearson, P. D., Clark, K., & Walpole, S. (1999). *Beating the odds in teaching all children to read* (Report #2-006). Ann Arbor, MI: Center for Improvement in Early Literacy Achievement.

Thomas, A., Fazio, L., & Stiefelmeyer, B. L. (1999). *Families at school: A guide for Educators.* Newark, DE: International Reading Association.

Tierney, R., & Readence, J. (2000). *Reading strategies and practices: A compendium* (5th ed.). Boston: Allyn & Bacon.

Topping, K. (1987). Paired reading: A powerful technique for parent use. *The Reading Teacher, 40*(7), 608–614.

Vacca, J., Vacca, R., Gove, M., Burkey, L., Lenhart, L., & McKeon, C. (2005). *Reading and learning to read* (6th ed.). Boston: Allyn & Bacon.

Waldbart, A., Meyers, B., & Meyers, J. (2006). Invitations to families in an early literacy support program. *International Reading Association,* 774–785.

Zutell, J., & Rasinski, T. V. (1991). Training teachers to attend to their students' oral reading fluency. *Theory to Practice, 30,* 211–217.

Index

Page numbers followed by an *f* or a *t* indicate figures or tables.

Supporting readers. *see also* Struggling
    readers
    guidelines for in-school independent
        reading and, 59–62
    with instructional routines, 62–74,
        70*f*
    overview, 16
Sustained silent reading (SSR), 9–10,
    72–74
Syntax, language. *see* Language syntax

T

Talking with children, home literacy
    and, 134–137
Tape-recorded reading, 71–72
Think-alouds, comprehension
    monitoring and, 105
Time to read
    daily reading time and, 23–24,
        25
    guidelines for in-school independent
        reading and, 60–61
    importance of, 19–22

starting early in the school year,
    25–27
sustained silent reading (SSR) and,
    9–10, 72–74
Troubleshooting during independent
    reading time, 53–57, 56*f*
Trust, importance of, 31–32

V

Vocabulary growth
    assessment of, 120–121
    classroom practices and, 92–94
    home literacy and, 134–137, 136*f*
    overview, 4–5, 4*f*

W

Whisper reading
    overview, 72
    during SSR, 73
Word family, 90–92
Word recognition
    assessment of, 114–116, 115*t*
    overview, 4–5, 4*f*
Workshops, parent, 143